"WHAT HAVE WE DONE?"

Jim Rusk with Kathie Rusk
"What Have We Done?"

Published by Spines
ISBN: 979-8-89383-116-0

"WHAT HAVE WE DONE?"

THE STORY OF ONE FAMILY'S CHALLENGES AND SUCCESSES IN THE NORTHWOODS OF MINNESOTA

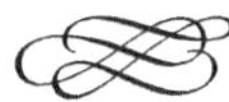

JIM RUSK WITH KATHIE RUSK

DEDICATION

To my wife, Kathie:

As you read this tale, you will understand her role in my life as my best friend and my total support. Without her, none of this would have been possible.

To our sons, Mike and Jim, and their families.

To all our friends and their families who provided us with support throughout our transition and adventures into a new life.

To anyone who reads this: Don't be afraid to follow your dreams.

CONTENTS

Preface   ix

Prologue   1
1. Part 1: Transition   13
2. Part 2: Arrival in Ely   27
3. Part 3: Mike   73
4. Part 4: Our Return Home   103
5. Part 5: 1993-2000   174
6. Part 6: "Is it Time to Sell?"   212
   Epilogue   245

PREFACE

In our first book, "Love You," Kathie and I chronicled 365 days of our military career. The time we were separated during my deployment to Vietnam. The book shared our love letters and recorded exchanges as I did my military duty while Kathie worked to raise our two young sons during my absence.

"What Have We Done?" follows our transition from our military career to our second career as owners and operators of Northern Lights Lodge in northern Minnesota for 19 years.

As we look back on our life, it's apparent that we have lived through four different phases: growing up, a military career, a second career, and retirement.

Our military career had been quite rewarding. Our boys were born in military hospitals in Massachusetts and Indiana. We had experienced life in Berlin, Germany for three years with two young children, the separation during my tour in Vietnam, two years of adventure in Addis Ababa, Ethiopia, and three wonderful years at Fort Lewis, Washington. Our sons, Mike, and Jim were young adults and looking forward to college.

It was now time to make hard decisions about what we were going to do after Jim's career in the military ended.

An opportunity came along to make dreams come true. We bought the Northern Lights Lodge on Bear Island Lake in Ely, Minnesota.

"What have we done?"

PROLOGUE

Should We Retire?

In 1981, I would complete twenty years of active duty, and the subject of retirement became an issue. Should we retire? When should we retire? What should we do when we retire? All these questions needed an answer. The easiest decision was to retire, and the hardest decision was what to do after retirement.

Michael had a very successful year in football his senior year, and he received numerous inquiries about football scholarships. Schools interested included Purdue University, Northwestern University, Miami of Ohio, and Ball State University. Kathie and I were able to accompany him on recruiting trips. A fun, exciting time. In early 1982, he was offered a "full ride" scholarship by Ball State University. It was a happy day for both him and his proud parents when he signed his letter of intent.

One option was to remain on active duty after my tour at Fort Harrison was over. Looking at my options, I concluded that most likely we could expect an assignment in Europe. This would have been OK for Kathie and me. I would probably end up commanding another finance office and fighting problems that I'd been fighting for the last 15 years. Mike was about to enter college, and Jim about to become a senior in high school. The thought of being in Europe while Mike was in the United States plus having to make Jim change schools in his senior year in high school made this option unattractive.

Many of my contemporaries were retiring and taking either federal jobs or jobs with corporations working on projects for the Federal Government. Because I was an officer in the regular Army, my retirement pay would be reduced if I took a job with the federal government, making that option unattractive.

One day I was looking at ads in the *Wall Street Journal*, and there was an ad offering a fishing resort for sale. Over the years, we had vacationed at various fish camps with the boys. We had often fantasized about owning such a business when we retired. Kathie and I talked about it and decided to investigate that option in more detail. I answered an ad by United Farms Realty asking them for information on resorts for sale anywhere in the United States. Soon the mail started pouring in. What fun, reading all the information on everything from small mom and pop fish camps to huge multimillion-dollar marinas. We used prices to determine what was within the range of possibility. Being familiar with Minnesota, we decided to visit some resorts that were listed for sale there. Little did we know what we were about to get ourselves into.

Minnesota had several small mom and pop resorts that catered to fisherman and families looking for a wilderness vacation with some of the comforts of home. Most resorts operated on a week-to-week basis as most vacations were taken in that manner. Separate cabins with kitchens, indoor "facilities," electricity, warm beds, and the opportunity to experience the famous woods and water of Minnesota's ten thousand lakes were key to selling the vacations. Most of the resorts operated in the summer, while a few were open year-round.

After scheduling appointments, we took a week's vacation at the end of October 1981 and headed for Minnesota. Our thinking was that we owed it to ourselves to at least investigate our dream just on the off chance that, just maybe, we could turn a dream into reality.

Minnesota Visit

We were particularly interested in the Arrowhead region. That term was used for the northeastern part of the state above Lake Superior. The economy of the area depended upon iron mining, tourism, and logging. The area was sparsely populated, heavily forested, and featured many of Minnesota's ten thousand lakes. The area also supported black bears, timber wolves, and moose.

Our first stop was Grand Rapids, about one hundred miles west of Ely where we had enjoyed many good vacations. For the next two days, we looked at two different resorts in the general area. Resort looking is more time-consuming than house hunting simply because of the distances between the various places for sale.

Right away, we learned that resorts went through a life cycle. Getting off to a fast start with a new owner, becoming more tired as business fails for whatever reason, and experiencing decay as the money runs out. Finally, the business is put up for sale. The places we saw fell into the final category. We were interested in a place with at least livable quarters for us. Neither resort offered good living accommodations.

Our next stop was the Orr area, which is about sixty miles northwest of the Ely location. Both places we saw there had potential. One had about a dozen cabins and a full bar with living quarters above the bar. I quickly decided that I was not the bartender type. The second one was on a small piece of ground, maybe four acres. It had two homes. One, the "mother-in-law place," was very nice. The second was a combination store, marina, and living quarters. It was in tough shape. A previous owner had trouble getting heat to flow to the second story, so he solved the problem by simply cutting a large hole in the floor, what a mess. It was raining the day we looked at the place and in four of the six cabins, water was running through the ceiling and the appliances were rusting out as we stood there. One cabin was sitting at a strange angle. The Realtor simply said, "Oh, you can jack that up without difficulty," Not!

It was Thursday evening, and we only had one day left on our trip. While we had nothing scheduled to see in Ely, we decided to spend our last day there for old times' sake. Ely was literally "at the end of the road," located a few miles south of the Canadian border and the border of the Boundary Waters Canoe Area. In the early 1900s, logging and mining had been the major activities in the area. The mines had closed, and the huge white pines had been logged out, leaving tourism as the major industry. The area boasted about 500 lakes within a twenty-mile radius of Ely. The town had a year-round population of about 3,500 but swelled to over 30,000 during the summer months. In addition to some 25 resorts, there were several outfitters renting canoes and camping gear. There was also a large Boy Scout base that allowed scouts to experience summer canoeing and winter adventures in the wilderness.

We had not been in Ely since before leaving for Ethiopia in1975. After we checked into the motel, Kathie said, "Let's call some Realtors and see if any resorts are for sale here." One had a place for sale on an island in a lake quite a distance away, and another had a place for sale about ten miles south of Ely. We made an appointment to see that place the next day.

Northern Lights Lodge

We met the realtor, Fred, who drove us to Northern Lights Lodge (NLL). The resort was located on Bear Island Lake about ten miles south of Ely and five miles north of Babbitt. I think all the stars were in alignment that morning. It was a beautiful clear day and the trees were in their full autumn display. As we drove in, there was a buck and doe standing at the top of the hill next to the resort house. NLL consisted of five summer cabins (one, two, and three bedrooms), an old garage, a boat house, and a small house. The house was about 900 square feet with two bedrooms, a living room, bath, and kitchen on the second floor. The first floor had a den with a fireplace and a garage which had been converted into a small bar by a previous owner.

The first thing that struck me was that the cabins were in reasonably good shape. It would not take a bunch of money to begin business, something each of the other resorts required. Another strong point was the cabins were spread over 1,100 feet of shoreline, quite large compared to the resorts we had looked at earlier. About ten acres were included with the resort. The place reminded both of us of Makie's Cabins, the first place we'd stayed at in Ely after my return from Vietnam in 1970. Quiet, a good distance between cabins, and lots of trees and water. WE WERE IN LOVE!

Bear Island Lake

Bear Island Lake was about 2,500 acres. It had been formed by glaciers millions of years ago and featured clean water, more than two miles long, and a mile wide. It had a wide variety of structure with depths varying from shallow bays to over 90 feet in the main lake. The water was "tea" colored, having been stained by tamarack pine trees that populated the area through which the inlet river flowed. The trees produced the stain. It was dotted with several islands. The largest, over 50 acres, had the shape of a bear – if you had enough to drink, thus its name. Only one island had cabins, and while there were homes and cabins located around the lake, it still had a wilderness feel. NLL was the smallest of three resorts on the lake. Bald eagles nested on one island, while loons and mergansers summered on the lake. There were also several active beaver lodges scattered around the lake. Fish included walleye, northern pike, small and largemouth bass, plus a variety of panfish. Ideal for our potential customers. The resort was located at the mouth of Bear Island River, the outlet river, and featured the best and largest sand beach on the lake.

The Purchase

Back at the realtor's office, we discovered that Fred and a partner, John, owned the resort. They were the third owner in the past three years. The story was that they had bought the place for one of Fred's sons to run, but he'd dropped out at the last minute, so it was currently being run by a local couple they hired to manage the resort. The former owner had put in the bar and lasted only one year. Earlier, the place had been called Coral Ridge Resort and had been operated successfully for several years by another local couple. Fred had renamed the resort Northern Lights Lodge.

The price was $165,000. Because of the high interest rates, places were being sold on Land Contracts. These were financed by the owners, and should the buyer fail to make payments, the resort would revert to the previous owner. Terms were $50,000 down, due January 1, 1982, with the balance spread over 20 years at 10 percent interest. After much discussion, we made the deal, paying the realtors $100 down and walked out the door. To this day, we firmly believe that they celebrated that night thinking that within a couple of years they would have the resort back plus our $50,000 down payment. We made a pledge to ourselves that this would never happen.

The next morning, we drove out of town, happy and concerned. We had to find the $50,000, plus determine how we were going to run the place starting just a few months later. Should I retire now? That would mean moving Jim to a new school, his senior year, something we didn't want to do. Should I stay on active duty until Jim graduates? How would we operate the resort that first year? All these questions needed answers, and we fell silent in our thoughts as we drove back to Indianapolis.

Back Home

When we got home, the boy's reaction to our announcement was, "Wow, you've finally done something crazy!" Mike's upcoming year was settled with his football scholarship to Ball State University, and it was obvious that Jim had no desire to leave before he graduated. His girlfriend was a year behind him in school, and they had "grand" plans for their future.

Earlier that year, we'd heard from our old Army friends, the Frydendahls, that Jerry was also about to retire. We had served with them in Ethiopia. They were about 10 years older but had a son and daughter about our boys' age, so the two families bonded. While Jerry was a full Colonel and I was a Major, rank played no role in our friendship. We enjoyed many fun times camping together. Kathie and JoAnn even opened a long-closed military library and were able to offer current books to members of our unit. On a whim, we called them and asked what they were doing next summer after Jerry retired? Explaining our purchase, we asked them if they'd like to spend the summer in Ely helping Kathie and the boys operate the resort while I remained on active duty. To our amazement, they said, "When do you want us to come?" Another problem solved.

My dad had passed away in 1980, and as part of his will, both boys were scheduled to receive $25,000. Due to legal requirements, the funds would not be available until the summer of 1982. I asked them if they'd be willing to "invest" that money into our resort to make the down payment. Both said, "Yes." However, to this day, I wonder if they said that because they wanted to or if I got that answer because I put undue pressure upon them. An answer I will never know. We also decided that Jim and I would return to Ely during the

Christmas break to borrow the necessary dollars to meet the January 1 deadline.

Winter in Ely

When Jim and I checked into the motel in Ely, it was about 25 degrees below zero, with about 20 inches of snow on the ground. A prediction of things to come. We drove to the resort and found that the previous owners had let the managers remain in the house without telling us. They were huddled together in the living room, trying to stay warm when we walked in. I offered to let them stay through the winter if they would pay for the utilities, but when they refused, I asked them to vacate the house immediately.

After long discussions with the manager of Northwest Bank in Ely, I managed to secure a six-month loan for $50,000 at 15 percent interest! The down payment was made to Fred and John, and they agreed to watch the place through the winter now that the managers had left.

Jim spent a great deal of time wading through the snow, taking pictures of the cabins from all angles, and shortly thereafter, we drove out of Ely as real resort owners.

PART 1: TRANSITION

The Spring of 1982

As we entered 1982, my time was spread between work and trying to figure out how we were going to find customers for the resort. My boss, Colonel Herb Gassie, and my co-workers were very interested in our venture, and Herb was especially helpful through the summer, allowing me to take extra time to travel to the resort.

In 1982, Sport Shows were a common way to advertise businesses like ours. We had nothing to set up a booth at the Indianapolis Sport Show but did spend several evenings at the show helping the Executive Director of the Ely Chamber of Commerce, Jeannie Larson. We would become great friends and remained in contact over the years until her passing. My reason for spending time at the show was to listen to what questions potential customers were asking. It was all part of trying to learn how to sell our resort. I always thought we could make a success of the business because of what we'd learned over the years from being customers at various resorts. This knowledge would guide us in the years to come.

We did not have one reservation on the books when we bought NLL; we had to start from scratch with everything. In April, we got our first deposit check, $50, and we went out to dinner to celebrate! How little did we know.

Our First Season

On the first of May, I took two weeks' vacation, and Kathie and I went to Ely. Jerry and JoAnn Frydendahl arrived with their trailer, which would be their home for the summer. John came to the resort and helped Jerry and me turn on the water, repairing many water lines in each cabin that had frozen and broken during the winter.

The Cabins

Kathie and JoAnn had great fun cleaning and working in the cabins. Cabins 1-4 were built around 1950 and were half-log sided with tar paper roofs. Cabin 5, the 3-

bedroom cabin, was built later as the bathroom was included in the interior design. Cabins 1-4 were not insulated, while #5 had limited insulation. The interiors were knotted pine walls, and the bathrooms for Cabins 1-4 were added after the original cabins were built. They had a commode, metal shower, sink, medicine cabinet, and hot water heater. The cabins had small heaters. The kitchens had white porcelain-coated cabinets and a one-piece counter/sink and cupboards that were also metal and coated with white porcelain. Each had a three-quarter size refrigerator with a small freezer unit inside the box. Propane gas stoves completed the kitchen. The stoves, heaters, and hot water heaters had pilot lights which needed to be lit and maintained. Electricity was provided through a fuse box, so each fuse had to be checked when the power was disrupted. The cabins had the basic kitchen utensils, bedding, etc., but everything needed to be inventoried and their condition checked. Lists were made for the needs of each cabin. Over time, each cabin was upgraded by replacing the fuse boxes with circuit breakers and the kitchen cabinets, countertops, and sinks.

Other Tasks

Jerry and I worked on getting the docks out, boats cleaned, lake water system turned on, etc. Early on, I decided that we needed a bulletin board outside for our guests. There was a small grove of trees separating our house from Cabin 5, an ideal location for the board. Jerry and I used a 4x8 foot sheet of plywood fastened to two birch poles, and we had it up and ready. It turned out to be a popular stop for our guests as we posted a schedule of events in Ely and then started taking photos of guests with their fish catches. Our little Polaroid camera worked perfectly. We would take two photos, putting one on the board and giving the other one to the guest. We also sent the photos to the local newspaper in Ely, which printed weekly pictures of guests and their fish. Another method of advertising.

We also learned about the much-heralded Minnesota insects. The State had done a great job advertising the mosquito population but failed to mention a little black bug that locals called "black flies". While not really a fly, their bite was significantly worse than a mosquito. My first encounter was weed whacking on the beach and feeling my forehead wet – thinking it was sweat I wiped it, and it was blood. Instead of sticking you with a needle like a mosquito, these bugs cut you. The mosquito bites usually went away in 24 hours while a black fly bite lasted a week or so. JoAnn even swelled up and ended up having to wear netting when she was outside. Fortunately, the flies only lasted about a month, mid-May to mid-June.

When my vacation was up, Kathie and I returned to Indianapolis to wait for the boys to finish school. School was out in late May and after Mike graduated from High School, Kathie and the boys set out for Ely in our van pulling our 14-foot fishing boat. They were almost to Duluth when a tire on the boat trailer blew, and they had quite a time getting it repaired. Thanks to help from some local folks, repairs were made, and they made it to Ely. Our plan was for me to work and then take long weekends to make periodic visits to the resort throughout the summer. I believe our first real business was housing a wedding group over the Memorial Day weekend. Slowly we were getting additional reservations for weeklong visits, mostly "spill over" business from resorts that were already full. Our first reservation was such a case, referred to us by our neighbor resort, The Escape.

Our lack of business was a good thing for everyone at the resort. It allowed time to prepare the cabins, and Jerry remained quite busy repairing a multitude of problems. He was quite a "handyman" which proved to be invaluable. I managed a couple of visits in June and took a week's leave in July to be there the first and only week of the summer that all our cabins were rented. My trips were 800 miles one way in our little Honda. I would make the drives in one very long - normally about 16 hours a day as time was critical. If there was a three-day weekend, Herb would give me another day off, so I'd have two days at the resort with two days of driving.

Bears and Birds

One day while I was working in Indianapolis, I received a letter from Kathie that had a couple of Polaroid photos. They were black! Kathie had a note on each saying they were pictures of "our" black bear! Our garbage can was near the back door, and on more than one occasion, a bear would come looking for a snack. It turned out that we were located on a 'bear highway' that led from the three resorts on the lake north for some three miles to the county's open garbage dump. The two other resorts had restaurants, so there were always ample pickings for the bears. We only had the cabin garbage cans, but the bears loved to grab the trash bags out of the cans and drag them out to enjoy whatever they could find. They especially loved the cans where guests had put their grease dripping from frying fish. A couple of years later, the country closed the open dump, converting it to a transfer point. This lowered the bear visits considerably.

We also enjoyed a large variety of birds and set out a few feeders. Our kitchen had large windows looking out over the road and down towards the garage and cabins. I built a large feeding station near the house which held eight different feeding stations, and we enjoyed many hours watching a wide variety of birds. The feeders also attracted our local pine squirrels and the bears. We set up a deer feeding trough and each winter watched the deer feed. Our first year we started putting out food when the first snow arrived and had a beautiful buck visit frequently. After hunting season was over, the buck did not reappear, so we decided not to start feeding until after hunting season.

One night while we were in bed, Kathie woke me saying that something just flew by her head. I laughed and tried to go back to sleep. Suddenly, something "whooshed" by my head. After turning on the lights, we found a bat hanging onto the drapes. I used a minnow dip net to successfully capture the bat and release him unharmed. They loved to eat mosquitoes! We decided that the bat was able to enter through the chimney of our fireplace. Over the years we had a few more visits. Part of our wilderness adventures! Field mice would also join us in the house. This usually happened in the fall when they were seeking warm shelter. We had traps set around and on occasion we would see one run across the base of our fireplace and a minute later hear a trap "ping!"

The Beach

The resort had an excellent beach that, over the years, had been formed by sand pushed onto shore along a point that jutted into the lake for about two hundred yards at the beginning of the outlet river. When the resort was transitioning between owners and not busy, many folks with cabins on the lake had used the beach. We could see their boats heading towards the beach full of beach toys, chairs, etc. It became a frequent task to go to the beach and tell everyone that new owners had arrived and that the beach was private property. While not happy, most left without incident. One day, I walked to the beach carrying a shotgun. The word must have gotten around as we no longer had a problem.

I managed to do a little fishing in our lake and caught a few fish. Jerry was not a good fisherman but made up for his lack of expertise by being a very lucky fisherman, and he would always catch more fish than me when we would take the boat down the river. The motors that came with the resort were in poor shape, and they were always a struggle to keep running when we had them rented to guests. When I returned to Indianapolis, I worked out a trade for two 5 horsepower motors. I traded a coin collection for them. It turned out that the motors were also not very trustworthy, and I had to replace them in the coming years.

In early August, I took Jim and Mike back with me to Indianapolis. Mike was starting football at Ball State and, shortly thereafter, Jim would start football practice for North Central High School. When we got home, we discovered that the house had been broken into. A few things had been taken and other items were stacked in the living room, but apparently the robbers were scared off by someone. We felt violated.

I returned to the resort after making sure the boys were settled in for their school activities. We were not full, so Kathie and I decided to spend nights in different cabins just to get to learn more about how they operated and what we needed to improve for our guests, etc. My first night there, we went down to our little one-bedroom cabin, #1, and settled in for the night. Shortly thereafter, Jerry knocked on the door and told us that I had an urgent phone call.

Ed

The call was from Sharon, Ed's wife, telling me that my brother Ed had died suddenly that evening. He was 47 and had spent the day getting ready to leave the next morning for Islamabad, Pakistan. He was a member of the Central Intelligence Agency (CIA). The Russians were fighting in Afghanistan, and the United States was supporting the Afghan rebels through Pakistan. Ed and I had talked earlier, and he had told me that he hoped he would be able to hike into Afghanistan with a group of rebels on a resupply mission. He had taken a nap and never awoke. Sharon never consented to an autopsy, so

I don't know why he died. I was very disappointed in her decision as our family has a history of strokes, heart attacks, and early deaths. Knowing why he died may have helped the rest of us.

I was stunned. Ed was almost five years older than me, and during our school years, we were not very close. As we got older, our relationship deepened, and as I looked back, I realized what a profound impact Ed had on my life. He went to military school because it was "cool," and I followed him. He graduated from Kent State University and so did I. He received his commission in the Army through ROTC at Kent and so did I. Dad had died a few months earlier and now Ed. In a few short months, my family had been eliminated. We hopped in the car, drove to Indianapolis to tell the boys what had happened. Then picked up clothes and went on to Washington, DC for the funeral. I was numb. Later in the fall, I returned to DC for Ed's burial with full military honors in Arlington National Cemetery. I remember standing at attention in full uniform as Taps was played with tears streaming down my face. Sharon and I were then invited to CIA Headquarters where in a brief ceremony, Ed was presented with two awards. We were thanked on behalf of the CIA and told the awards could not be made public and would remain with the Agency.

Our First Year

In mid-September, I returned to NLL for the last time to close everything for the winter. Our water lines were buried close to the surface and would freeze if the system was not closed. The cabins were not insulated so "mother nature" ended our season by the end of September.

We had made it despite everything. Our year was rather meager. We'd managed to rent 27 cabin weeks out of a potential of about 100 weeks. Nothing to brag about, and we had collected just over $9,000 in rent. Enough to make the first year's payment, but that payment would jump to over $15,000 the next year so we had our work cut out for us. We had spent the summer taking pictures, and one goal during the coming winter was to redesign and produce a new four-color brochure. The one we had inherited with the business was two-color, white and brown - not representative of the beautiful blue lakes and green forests! Jerry said he'd probably go to work during the winter but that he would take some time the following spring to return and help us reopen the resort. They were unbelievably wonderful friends.

The End of my Army Career

That fall, Mike learned that he would be "red-shirted"

for his freshman year. He was somewhat disappointed, but by being red-shirted, he gained an extra year of eligibility, which shortly would become very important. He did win a team award for the most improved freshmen lineman. Jim had a very successful year in football, making many "highlight reel" blocks during his games. North Central again lost to archrival Carmel in the playoffs. Jim did not receive the scholarship attention that Mike had. It was a question of size rather than ability. Jim just wasn't big enough to become a college lineman. Mike did well in school and decided to major in computer science, a challenging field. Jim had a happy senior year, enjoying his friends and girlfriend and remaining content with his "C's".

We did get our new brochure printed in time for us to distribute it at the 1983 Indianapolis Sport Show. Putting the four-color brochure together was an exciting project. We had taken many pictures of the cabins and the lake, and I remember needing a "fishing" picture. We accomplished this by having me, Mike, and Bob in the boat. I was holding the fishing rod - bent double - and Mike splashed the water with a net as he netted the "big one."

It was an exciting time being a business owner at the ten-day Sport Show and talking with many people. We were starting to learn the business and were able to book some reservations for the upcoming season. Our new brochure was also producing results as we sent them to potential customers that had contacted the Ely Chamber of Commerce, and we were getting repeat reservations from folks who had stayed with us the first year. Things were looking up for NLL.

Work went well and in early 1983, I officially submitted my retirement papers asking to be released from Active Duty on June 1, 1983. The request was approved, and we started making plans to leave Indianapolis after Jim's graduation in May. Arrangements were made to put the house up for sale. Selling the house turned out to be quite a struggle with mortgage interest rates hovering around 17 percent. We finally found a buyer who was able to assume our 11 percent VA loan. We lost money on the sale. We arranged to have our household goods shipped to Ely. Our last move at Government expense.

I received a Legion of Merit on retirement, a very high military award with great satisfaction. The traditional retirement gift for retiring officers was some sort of silver serving dish engraved with the officers' name and dates of service. I asked for and received a chain saw! A fitting conclusion to my career.

We left Indianapolis, excited about our new career, not understanding the challenges that lay ahead for everyone.

Looking Back

Our time in the Army had been wonderful and very rewarding. Many challenges were faced, many problems overcome, and much, much enjoyment experienced. The critical date in my mind was April 28, 1962, the day I married Kathie. Her support and love gave me the extra confidence that I would need over the years to become successful. We made many solid friends, some of whom would be destined to play large roles in our future. We still enjoy visiting with these friends whenever the opportunity presents itself.

PART 2: ARRIVAL IN ELY

Arrival

While my official retirement date was June 30, 1983, I had accumulated 60 days of terminal vacation, so we left in early May for Ely. Jerry and JoAnn had agreed to return for a month to help us open the resort. Prior to our departure, we celebrated Jim's graduation from high school. When our household goods were packed, we urged the moving company not to use a customary 18-wheeler for the move due to our small, long road into the resort.

Upon our arrival in Ely, all efforts were devoted towards getting the resort open for business. Jerry and I learned hard lessons about how poorly we had done closing the previous fall as water sprayed from many leaks created by frozen water lines in each cabin.

Mother Nature allowed us no slack, and each little area in a copper pipe which held water during the winter was broken. Each cabin had a crawl space underneath, and the area was a maze of flexible copper pipes for the well water system and the lake water system. The pipes were bent around each other, and the connections fitted together in a haphazard fashion. Previous owners had used whatever connections were available so there was no set pattern or drains for the water.

Each dip or bend in the pipe presented a potential problem if the water was not completely drained when the cabin was closed for the season. Our one-bedroom cabin had a hole about two feet deep that provided access to the water lines. You had to lay on your back to hook up the lines with barely enough room for the two crescent wrenches needed for the job. I soon learned how poor at soldering I was, especially when the copper pipes were wet. You used the solder by heating it and the pipe with a blowtorch. When the solder melted, it would flow into the split, harden, and fix the leak.

Unfortunately, I had a habit of setting the wood around the pipe on fire before the solder melted. We were soon counting the number of leaks per cabin - happy when we only encountered three or four. The process was long, difficult, and at times frustrating. Happiness was only achieved when the hot water tank started to fill and there were no drips or spraying water underneath the cabin.

While we were working on the water, Kathie and JoAnn went about the business of cleaning the cabins, washing windows, vacuuming walls and floors, making beds and once we had hot water, washing dishes. We called it "waking up the cabins after a long winter's nap!"

Shortly after our arrival, over the hill came a huge 18-wheeler with our household goods. What a sight. Somehow the driver managed to get the rig turned around and he, along with Mike and Jim, unloaded everything into the house. It took all day, but we finally moved in.

An old beat-up truck had come with the resort, and we were finally able to get it to run. If memory serves me right, it was a '67 Chevy pickup with the bed nearly rusted out. Somehow it made it to the dump a couple of times, and Jim dearly loved to drive it even when the wheels didn't want to turn when you turned the steering wheel. Obviously, we needed to find a pickup for our daily chores. The boys painted the old truck with house paint, and we even put eyes and big red teeth on the grill - what a sight driving the three miles to the dump!

A couple of weeks later, Jerry and JoAnn had to leave for Texas. Jerry had accepted a job with a government contractor working on Army missiles at Fort Bliss. It was a sad day when they left. I was especially concerned as I had leaned heavily on Jerry for help in solving maintenance problems and the thought of being on my own was scary. I had spent most of my Army career behind a desk and now I would be expected to solve problems as they were encountered by our guests. Somehow, I would have to learn to do handyman jobs which I knew nothing about. While in the Army, the motto of the Finance Corps was, "Learn to do by Doing," and that's exactly what happened to me as I learned how to resolve these problems over the years.

Jim and Mike were a huge help throughout the process of opening the resort. Without them, getting the docks out, boats in the water, motors running would have been a most difficult task. The grounds also needed a lot of attention after the long winter. Slowly but surely, piece by piece, the resort started to take shape. While fishing season opened in the middle of May, our first customers usually didn't start to arrive until the Memorial Day weekend.

Bob

The boys had always wanted us to get a bigger dog. We had dachshunds since we were married and arrived at the resort with Ralf and Max. My answer had always been, "When we have more space, we'll get a bigger dog." Soon after the moving van had left, the boys said let's get a big dog. That day the local paper, *The Ely Echo*, had printed pictures of a couple of dogs up for adoption at the local vet. The boys took off to Ely to look them over. When they left, I knew that another dog was in our future. Sure enough, they returned with this reddish-brown and white pup that was all legs and feet. After much discussion, we settled on the name "Bob" after the clay character that was then popular on the David Letterman show. He was a welcome addition to the family and was soon bounding all over the resort being chased by Ralf and Max.

Bob soon grew to be a 50-plus pound animal, friendly and full of energy. He seemed to understand that he had been saved and would prove to be an asset to us and the business. While he was our first "All American" dog, he was by far our most stable and dependable friend over the coming years. I will mention him frequently in the coming pages.

The Business

From the day we bought the resort, I always had confidence that we would be successful. While I was probably very naive, I never doubted our decision. We had made the purchase based on our "heart" rather than our "head." While my accounting background allowed me to calculate in my head what was needed to generate sufficient revenue to make the payments, etc., I did not understand the finer points of the business. Had I gone to a banker and asked for a formal financial analysis, I am sure that I would have been told that the purchase was unwise. During our first year, Jerry had kept track of our income and expenses. Based on our first year's performance, he told JoAnn as they drove out of the resort at the end of that year, that we would never make a go of the business.

Factors weighing against our decision included: We were the third owner in three years. The previous two owners had destroyed any "goodwill" associated with the business due to their lack of attention. We bought the resort with no reservations in the books, not a good sign. The average resort owner in Northeastern Minnesota managed to stay in business for less than five years. Once we were settled in and really looked in detail at the resort, we found many infrastructure problems. Each cabin had its own septic system, and some would require updating and enlarging. The docks were in very poor condition - something you don't see when they are buried in snow. The water system was fragile. Drinking water came from a shallow well and there were two other sand point wells not in operation. Commode water came from a lake water system which consisted of a long hose out into the lake connected to a pump and holding tank. It was a great idea and helped lessen the impact on the main drinking water well. Each cabin had a separate water hookup for the commodes. It was great when we heard them starting to fill. The boats were okay, but most had slow leaks and the outboard motors were in very poor condition. When you added up everything, it was obvious that a lot of money would be needed in future years to overcome these shortcomings.

On the positive side, we had our Army retirement check coming in each month. This provided about $2,000 each month to pay for our food, clothing, insurance, medical, etc. This would allow us to plow whatever we made back into the business. Looking back, without the Army retirement benefits, we could not have been a success. Our new brochure was a huge success and it allowed us to become competitive with other businesses. Our main source of leads for customers were inquiries received by the Ely Chamber of Commerce.

As part of our membership dues, we received a list of inquiries twice a week. We never delayed in sending our brochures and were constantly "attached" to our telephone to answer questions and hopefully book reservations. Our phone was connected to a bell which rang outside and many times we'd race from whatever we were doing into the house to answer the phone. In the 1980s, before the internet/emails/smartphones, the landline telephone was our lifeline. Both of us soon learned that we were able to "sell" our business over the phone. We loved our place and were confident that we could provide our customers with a positive vacation experience which made selling easier.

Probably the single most important factor in operating a resort is to understand that it was a business and must be treated as such no matter what. Over the years, so many people would tell us that they wanted to own a resort because they loved to hunt and fish. I would always laugh at the comment because my fishing time dropped to almost zero while the resort was open. My time was required to serve the customer and maintain the business.

During the main season, it was a happy time as a great deal of money would be flowing in. Unfortunately, that season only lasted if you were lucky, maybe sixteen weeks. This left 36 weeks with no dollars flowing in. We found that a great deal of discipline was needed to manage the money to ensure your financial obligations could be met throughout the year. I believe our many years in the Army where we were only paid once a month had taught us this high level of discipline needed to successfully manage the business. In the early part of the season, our dollars were put directly into savings until we had accumulated enough to make our annual resort payment. We had made that vow to each other that we'd never miss a payment and lose the resort to the previous owners.

Understanding that the "customer always comes first" was also important for success. Back when we were customers, we remembered how we felt when some piece of equipment failed to work or the times, we'd go to the office seeking information only to find a sign on the door saying the owner would be back in a few hours. Our goal was always to prevent our customers from having similar poor feelings towards us. This meant that for the months of June through August, we never went to town together or out to dinner or fishing together. While we were together constantly, many times we were not together as one of us always needed to be there should a customer needed something.

Another key factor in the business was generating goodwill which, in turn, created repeat business. Each year we needed between 75 and 100 cabin weeks to meet our financial responsibilities. Each week of repeat business was one less new customer we had to find. At times, this created problems in that some customers would want a set time each year. I found that it was too risky to hold weeks open, hoping this year's customer would want the same time next year. Therefore, we adopted a first come/first served policy for reservations. This did create some problems as it would on occasion cause some hard feelings when a customer found that the week/s they wanted the following year had already been booked. We would usually raise rates each year but always tried to make some type of improvement to justify the increase. I believe our repeat customers appreciated this as for the most part they willingly accepted the increases.

I think one of our biggest decisions on problems was where and how to spend our advertising dollars. Advertising was extremely expensive for our little business plus totally unpredictable as to how effective it would be. Our most effective advertising was with the Ely Chamber of Commerce. In addition to the prospect lists I've already mentioned, we would participate in group ads sponsored by the Chamber. Over the years, we also did some print advertising in various publications, usually with little or no success.

Another major advertising tool was the Sport Show. In the 1980s and until the mid-1990s ,sport shows were the major way the public could find resorts like ours. Visiting shows allowed the public to search out facilities in various parts of the country, talk directly to the owners and book vacations. Once the Internet took hold, the importance of the shows diminished. Our major show was the Indianapolis Boat, Sport and Travel Show held each February. We participated in that show for some 15 years and always did well. We also attended another show in Minneapolis for a few years but never had much success there.

I have spent time relating some of our business experiences here to give the reader a small sense of some of the factors we needed to be successful at to make Northern Lights a viable business.

Our First Year - Full Time

1983 was a happy year. We got the business going, and we were able to about double what we had done in 1982. Nothing to brag about, but in my mind, a very positive indicator that we could be successful. It turned into a very eventful year as we learned more about the business and attempted to learn more about the people and communities near us, Ely, and Babbitt. After so many moves in the Army, we were confident that we'd found our home and things would be stable for years to come. Little did we know.

The Guide

In addition to getting the physical side of the resort ready for business, I realized that I needed to learn everything I could about the lake so that I could respond to our guests' questions. With a map of the lake and either Jim or Mike, I tried to spend time on the lake just figuring out the layout, depths, etc. After running the boat up on a large rock one afternoon while investigating a floating jug, we learned jugs meant rocks! I was a mid-western bass fisherman, and we were soon able to find and catch decent bass, particularly in the outlet river which started at our point. Unfortunately, fishing in Minnesota meant walleyes, a fish I'd never been able to catch. Before I could talk to guests about that type of fishing, I needed to know what to do.

My problem was solved one day just after we had arrived when a guy in a beat-up old truck drove into the resort. It was Denny Meyers from Babbitt who asked if he could guide our guests on fishing trips. I'd never thought about such a thing but decided that I would hire him to guide me around the lake and teach me how to fish for walleyes. You can learn a lot about a person when you fish with him and I soon learned that Denny really did know how to catch walleyes, and we became good friends. To find customers, Denny agreed to teach a fishing seminar each Sunday evening. He would talk in detail about walleye fishing and solicit business. The seminars were an immediate hit and I continued them for many years to come.

Soon we all became good friends with Denny's wife Connie and their two young girls, Rochelle, and Shannon. They were our first friends in the Babbitt area. In addition to guiding, Denny also helped on occasion around the resort and was very involved with our decision to buy a couple of snowmobiles that winter. They were also the first couple we had known that were on welfare. Denny loved to smoke so I would pay him at times with groceries instead of dollars, so he wouldn't spend the money on cigarettes.

Denny was also taking courses in wilderness management at Vermilion Community College in Ely. Working together we plotted out several nature trails around the property. Denny would do core samples of some of the larger trees, and I would write a description of the species and list its age, etc., and set up a signpost. The trails became very popular with our guests. On a sad note, one day Denny was brushing one of the trails with his dog, Jake, a large black lab. As he was swinging the cutter back and forth, Jake got hit, and we lost him that day.

Power

Power was an issue. Power was provided to each cabin from lines attached to poles running throughout the resort. We soon discovered that on some occasions when the winds were strong, power would be interrupted to various cabins. The poles were rotting off at the ground, and they would swing back and forth in the wind. I'm sure that at times, the power lines held up poles rather than the other way around! We hired an electrician to come and put the power underground to Cabins 1 - 4, those that were encountering the problems.

We also ran power to the docks for these cabins, which allowed our guests to recharge trolling motors without having to lug their batteries up to the cabins. The electrician used a mechanical trencher to dig in the lines. I thought I knew where the water/propane lines ran, but the trencher soon proved me wrong. Before it was over, we'd cut three water lines and four gas lines. As the electrician dug the trenches, we followed behind him repairing the water lines and propane lines. Despite all of this, it was a great relief to have the power underground for that part of the resort.

Extra Land

One day that summer, as we were driving out to the main road, we encountered a group of surveyors working along the road. When I asked what was happening, they told me the owners were surveying lots to sell off. As I mentioned earlier, our place included 10 acres with the property line next to our house. I was immediately concerned about maintaining our privacy and the wilderness aspect around the resort - something we were selling. The land was owned by Fred and John, from whom we bought the resort. We met to discuss buying the land and finally agreed to buy an additional 60 acres for $70,000. This included everything except for five acres near the main road (Highway 21) which Fred said he'd promised the church. We accepted the deal which required us to pay for the land in ten years versus the 20 years for the resort at the same interest rate of 10 percent. It later became obvious that this had been their plan from the start to hopefully force us into a second sale. It worked. Kathie didn't say anything at the time but later admitted that she was not happy that we'd taken on the extra responsibility for these payments.

We now owned 70 acres, and our private road was 0.6 miles long. The additional property added over 600 feet of shoreline down Bear Island River which made the purchase a wise decision.

Fall

In mid-August, Mike returned to Ball State to start football practice. His season always started with a physical test, and if players did not do well on the test, they were in big trouble with the coaching staff. Mike lifted weights in our garage and did some running before he left. When he'd run down Highway 21, I would drive alongside, yelling at him to run faster. He was very upset by this, and I think very happy to leave for Ball State when the time came.

Jim had agreed to attend Vermilion Community College (VCC) in Ely for one year. His plan was to transfer to Indiana University for the '84 - '85 year to be with his current girlfriend, Lisa, who was a year behind him in school. He also decided to continue with football and joined the VCC squad. He started at tackle, and we enjoyed traveling around the area watching him play.

VCC had also advertised for part-time instructors. I applied and was accepted for one of the temporary positions. In September, I began teaching Business Machines and Typing. Quite a change from accounting, but it kept me busy, allowing me to meet more people in Ely and earn a few dollars.

Fall was a beautiful time of year. Our road had small maples, aspen, and pine trees, and it was amazing to watch the colors explode in the fall. There were lots of grouse, and Bob would love to walk with us along the road, hunting for grouse and scaring us to death when they exploded in flight out of the brush. I got the cabins closed for the winter, draining the water the best way I knew how. I found that I had to use an air compressor to blow the lines. This meant taking apart the systems by disconnecting the plumbing both inside the cabin and underneath each cabin. The compressor would blow, and the water would fly out. It would be next spring before I would learn if I had done a good job. We decided to leave Cabin 5, our 3-bedroom cabin next to the house, open for the winter as the previous owners had assured us that it was well-insulated and had been rented many times in the winter. As October faded, winter was right around the corner.

Al

Kathie's dad, Al, had been sick for several years with heart problems. They had begun many years earlier with a series of heart attacks, and he had even undergone one of the earliest heart bypass surgeries. However, that fall, things turned for the worse and in October, we received a call that he was near death. Kathie managed to get a flight out of Duluth and arrived by his bedside before he passed away. Jim and I drove to Indianapolis, picked up Mike from Ball State, and continued to Cleveland for the funeral. We all felt bad for Al. He'd worked hard his entire life, raised a wonderful daughter, but died a bitter person. Afterwards, we often wondered if some of his feelings were caused by his medication. He died unhappy with the way life, in his mind, had treated him. In his last years, he expressed this unhappiness by lashing out at those who loved and cared for him.

After the funeral, Jim, Mike, and I returned to Ball State while Kathie remained in Cleveland for a couple of weeks to be with her mom. These events gave me the opportunity to see Mike play in a football game for Ball State. The game was against Indiana State, and Mike played on Special Teams. On the first kickoff, he was penalized for roughing and never played anymore in the game. Later Kathie got to watch Ball State play Kent State in Kent, Ohio, but Mike was still warming the bench and did not play. After Mike's game, Jim and I returned to Ely.

Winter was rapidly closing in on Ely when Kathie returned from Cleveland.

Our First Winter

Winter in northeastern Minnesota begins early and lasts late. We had replaced the old truck with a Dodge pickup equipped with a plow and felt confident we could handle almost anything. I used the van to go to work, and Jim used the truck for school, while Mike had the Honda back at Ball State. As the temperatures dropped, we discovered that the propane hot water system for the house did a very poor job keeping the downstairs warm. The downstairs consisted of the office, a converted garage, and the den. Each had a small radiator, which did little to help warm things. The front of the garage had no insulation, and the door was a simple screen door, which also offered no protection from the elements. To help solve the problem, we built a temporary plywood wall for this entrance and filled the dead space with insulation. It helped a great deal but didn't solve the problem.

There was also a barrel stove in the basement. It was just as the name implied, a 30-gallon metal barrel laying on its side with a pipe connected to the furnace flu. Around the barrel was a sheet metal cover designed to trap the heat generated by the stove with a pipe leading to a vent upstairs. Never having used wood for heating, we decided to simply collect dead trees lying about the property, cut them up, and burn them. Sounded good but certainly did not work as well as it sounded. Unfortunately, such wood is still far from being dry, and much of it wouldn't start and, if it did, would produce more smoke than heat. The space around the stove was very limited, and we'd all end up with soot-covered faces as we tried to get the fire started. On those days when we were able to have a good fire, the system worked quite well. We also learned that heat from wood was much warmer than any heat generated by the furnace.

As November passed, we started picking up occasional snows of one to three inches and managed to keep our long road open without much difficulty. Our road was long, narrow, and full of dips, turns, and many places where a truck, even with 4-wheel drive and a plow, could become stuck. On the day before Thanksgiving, I walked out of VCC after finishing my last class, and the snow was really coming down. I knew that due to its light rear end, the van was not a good snow vehicle but had no choice but to head for home. The drive consisted of ten miles of country road to our place. Once I'd left Ely, the road turned into a track, and my only chance of making it was to keep up my momentum and hope that I did not end up in a ditch. Even though it was early afternoon, the sky was gray, no one was on the road, and the snow was building by the minute. Somehow, I made it to our road, and fortunately Jim had gotten home earlier and had already started plowing, and I managed to make it to the house. We got over 20 inches that day but were able to go to Babbitt (only five miles) to get the fixings for Thanksgiving dinner plus a cake we'd ordered for Jim's birthday celebration. We put the bags in the back of the truck and then had to dig them out once we got home as the snow was falling so hard. Jim or I plowed the entire weekend as we received an additional 20 inches on Thanksgiving. Jim's girlfriend, Lisa, from Indianapolis was visiting at the time, and we all had a great Thanksgiving and celebration of Jim's 19th birthday.

We learned that weekend that we had to plow continuously as the truck could only handle three to four inches of snow. Had we slept in and let the storm pass, we would never have made it out. With that much snow, the road became like a white tunnel, leaving very little room for error. More than once, we found ourselves digging out after becoming stuck. A snow shovel became part of the van and truck.

The heavy snow did provide us with the opportunity to use our snowmobiles. Denny had helped me pick out two matching Polaris machines. While they were not the top of the line, they were well-powered and could easily run 60 mph, even with me on board. I soon discovered that I had trouble staying on board, while Kathie and Jim were naturals at riding them. The neighbor resort staked out a route across the lake once the ice was safe. This allowed snowmobilers to travel safely over the ice to reach the groomed trails, which were at the far end of the lake.

As Christmas approached, Jim and I started making plans to redo the basement. A previous owner had installed a bar in the garage, and we decided to panel the walls, paint the floor, and turn the garage into our office. We would start the project after the Christmas holidays.

In mid-December, the weather forecast was for a low of minus thirty degrees. We were rather skeptical about it becoming that cold, but sure enough, we awoke the next morning to -30. It was a beautiful clear day, wonderful blue sky, and no wind. Another lesson, with the snow and these calm conditions, the bottom simply drops out of the thermometer. As I mentioned earlier, we were keeping Cabin 5 open hoping for some business. So far none had materialized. Each day we'd walk by the cabin listening to the heater cranking away. This morning because of the cold we went into the cabin. What a sight greeted us. The night before we had started a trickle of water in the kitchen and bath, a technique commonly used for cold weather in Indiana. The kitchen was still trickling away as it was about 5 feet from the heater. The bathroom was another story. The sink was at a 45-degree angle, filled with a block of ice and no water trickling. The commode water was frozen, and the tank water about 80 percent frozen. We went out of the winter business that day. I tried to drain the water, but we would pay a heavy price in broken pipes the next spring due to our decision to keep the cabin open.

As the winter progressed, -30 became the norm rather than the exception, and our education on Minnesota winters continued. We found that we had a lot to learn about cold weather. Just keeping the vehicles in running order required that we install block heaters and keep the truck and van "plugged in" overnight. On occasion, we would find that our tires had gone flat because the valves had frozen. Thankfully, our air compressor solved this problem. Footwear was also a challenge. Our hiking boots could not keep our feet warm, and we were introduced to Sorel insulated boots. Kathie hated them as they were brown, big, and generally ugly, but the felt inserts did the job and kept our feet warm.

While all of this was going on, Mike had found a wonderful girlfriend at Ball State. She was a junior, named Mitch. He wanted to bring her to our place for Christmas. Arrangements were made for them to fly into Duluth. They would arrive at 10 p.m. a couple of days before Christmas. Duluth was 100 miles south of Ely, and the day they were arriving the low was forecast to be -35. Fortunately, we only had to contend with the cold as it didn't snow when it is that cold. The kids arrived on schedule, and everyone huddled underneath blankets for the long trip home. We made it, happy to be home. As everyone settled in for the night, we discovered that we had no water.

The next morning there was still no water, and the temp outside was about -30. Our pump for the well was located down near the lake in a pit some four feet underground. The pit was covered with a heavy wooden top and the boys, and I went down and opened the pit to try to see what had happened. While we didn't know it at the time by opening the pit, we simply added insult to injury as all the cold air simply fell into the pit freezing everything even harder. Not knowing what to do, I called the original owner of the resort asking for help. He was very nice, giving up his day to come out and help. The final solution was a space heater lowered into the pit once we had determined that the pump, etc., were in operating order. Finally, later that afternoon, water came on to the great relief of five people in a small house with one bathroom. Another lesson learned. In the coming years, we learned to pile a layer of straw on the pit cover and place a 60-watt light bulb into the pit which kept the air above freezing throughout the winter. The rest of Mitch's visit went well, and we all celebrated the pending arrival of 1984.

Dorothy Molter

Dorothy was a legend in Ely. For many years, she had welcomed canoeists to her cabin, located in the newly created Boundary Waters Canoe Wilderness Area (BWCA), north of Ely. Her cabin was on an island in Knife Lake, some 25 miles northeast of Ely. She was a retired nurse from Indiana and would provide a welcome rest stop for canoeists passing by. She even sold homemade root beer and became known as the "Root Beer Lady."

The new area was managed by the US Forest Service, and once the law creating the area went into effect, resorts and private dwellings were bought out and removed. The law allowed Dorothy to remain in her cabin until she passed. Folks would bring her supplies on the snowmobiles. On January 1, 1984, snowmobiles were banned in the BWCA. As a result, folks in northeastern Minnesota decided to make one last visit to Dorothy on December 31, 1983. My guide, Denny, invited me to join him and another friend to make the trip. Denny rode Kathie's machine, and after towing the sleds some twenty miles north, we started the trip on Moose Lake. Being new to snowmobile riding, Denny promised me that he would only go as fast as I did. That promise lasted about two minutes as he and his friend disappeared in a cloud of snow. I had no choice but to try and stay with them. The ride was mostly over frozen lakes, but we also had to cross overland portages. At each portage, there were crowds of riders, celebrating, drinking, and generally having fun. I lost count of how many times I fell off the sled. Finally, we arrived at Dorothy's cabin. There were at least 100 machines lined up. We all went to the cabin to greet Dorothy and receive a hot cup of coffee and a cookie. What an experience.

When we were finished, Denny said they were going up the lake to visit another cabin. It too had been occupied by another long timer, but he had perished when the cabin burned. Zoom, off they went, and again I had no choice but to keep them in sight. Having reached the cabin site, we then started our return trip. I was introduced to slush fields, water standing on top of the ice. To navigate these areas, you had to keep the throttle wide open to skim over the water. If you slowed, you would become stuck. As we returned through the portages, the parties were louder and wilder as the liquid refreshments were taking a toll. The best sight was that of my truck at the end of the trip. Sometime later, Denny admitted to me that he and his buddy had tried to get me lost. Guess it was a type of initiation to northern Minnesota. I had passed the test without knowing it.

When Dorothy passed, the community of Ely moved her cabin, log by log, to the city, and it is now a museum honoring her. They even sell root beer.

1984

The year started normally, with Mike and Jim in school. I learned that my teaching job would end in late January, as my temporary space had been cut. That didn't bother me, as we had made reservations to attend the Sport Show in Indianapolis in late February, and I needed the time to prepare for the show. Jim and I, along with some help from Denny, started work on redoing the basement.

Northern Lights

We also experienced our first encounter with Northern Lights. One evening we were returning from Ely. It was a clear, cold evening and as we came around a turn in the road, the sky suddenly was ablaze with green and yellow stripes dancing in front of us. For a moment I thought I was hallucinating and then realized that we were viewing our first Northern Lights. Over the years, we enjoyed similar encounters. Sometimes green and yellow, other times with reds included. Many of our guests questioned us about seeing the Northern Lights, thanks to our name, and we could share our experiences with them.

The Sewing Club

One of the hardest things to do living out in the woods was making friends with residents. Teaching had helped, and doing business with local businesses allowed us to make connections, but not much on a personal basis. We were doing business with a local couple who owned Duane's Outfitters in Babbitt, Duane and Elsie Arvola. In addition to outfitting, they sold boats and motors. Kathie and Elsie shared experiences about cleaning cabins and just learning about the Northwoods. Elsie invited Kathie to her sewing club one day. The group was meeting that evening at Elsie's home.

It was a cold night, and after much discussion and encouragement, I managed to convince Kathie to go. She was reluctant, not knowing anyone. Off she went in the plow truck. A few minutes later she reappeared, cold, shaken, and upset. The truck was stuck, and she had to walk about a half mile back in the cold. We returned to the truck and sure enough, the plow blade was buried in a snowbank created from our plowing. After some shoveling, the truck was free, and after much discussion, Kathie left for the meeting.

The meeting turned out to be a great success for Kathie. There were about ten ladies in the club. They mostly socialized and did very little sewing. This one get-together opened the door for Kathie, and the friends she made that night became lifelong friends.

Over the years, they became well-known for their pranks and fun times. An example: To help one member celebrate her 50th birthday, they each brought a cake with 50 candles. They then had the Fire Chief come and arrest her for posing a fire threat to the community. On another occasion, a member got remarried but kept the wedding to a family-only celebration. Club members knew the reception was at a local café, so everyone appeared dressed in their elegantly distasteful outfits and kidnapped the groom, driving him around town in our van. Kathie's outfit was a black dress, calf-length red nylons, and heavy red lipstick, topped off with a large black lacy hat. Never a dull moment with the ladies of the sewing club when they got together.

Audie and Carol

During this time, we also made friends with Audie and Carol Austreng. We had attended a few meetings of the Babbitt Chamber of Commerce and had first met Carol there. She and Audie owned and operated the Babbitt Weekly News and the *Ely Miner*, both weekly newspapers. My first meeting with Audie was rather comical. For some reason, he drove into the resort in his big old car—I don't remember the make—and promptly got stuck in the snow. Not recognizing the car and watching from the kitchen window, I let out a curse, for there was another stranger I would have to dig out of a snowbank. It was not my most favorite task. Out climbs this little man, all 5'4", and we became lifelong friends. Shortly after we met, Audie agreed to let me write a column for the Babbitt paper. I called it the "Outside View." All newcomers were considered outsiders by the local residents in the communities. I decided to use the pseudonym "The Perch" for the articles because whenever I fished with Denny, he would catch walleyes and I'd catch perch. Later, our relationship with the Austrengs would become even closer.

Jim also received notice from Indiana University that his application for admission had been turned down. Two factors had worked against his application. One, he was now an out-of-state student, and two, his mediocre grades were not good enough. He was bummed out by the decision.

Our First Sport Show

We spent a lot of time getting organized for the upcoming Sport Show. Our booth was a 9 x 12 foot piece of concrete floor. Tables, decorations, etc., were our responsibility. Having the van, we could haul a lot of things and finally decided to make a background of birch logs with our resort sign in the middle. We also took a couple of fish mounts, boxes of brochures, and 1984 price lists. Our old friends from the Finance School, Nev and Jane Holder, offered us a place to stay during the show. Nev and I were assigned as accounting instructors at the school and became close friends. Jane and Kathie also became close, and they had a son and daughter about the same age as our boys.

Prior to the start of the show, we decided to spend Easter with Kathie's mom in Cleveland. It was the first time we'd visited Hilda since Al passed away. Mike and Mitch traveled up from Ball State to join us. During the visit, Mike suffered a deep headache, enough to put him into bed, which for him was most unusual. It was flu season, and we treated the symptoms accordingly. When he returned to school, Mike visited the clinic and was told that the type of flu on campus included headaches, so we all assumed that the cause was the flu.

Little did we know that this would turn out to be a signal of things to come.

The Sport Show lasted ten days covering two weekends. The key to a show was to have a booth in a high traffic area. Being a first-time customer, we ended up in a hallway that connected two of the larger buildings together, not the best, but the price a business paid for being new. Later we were able to move onto the main floor of the show, to a much better location. I think we did manage to book at least one reservation that year, but it was a great learning experience. We learned the types of questions people wanted answered, methods for how to get people to stop and talk especially on slow days, and most importantly that we could sell our place. We also met several other exhibitors and learned a great deal simply by exchanging experiences with each other.

The folks next to us were also from Indiana and owned a similar place in Canada. We shared lots of stories especially when business was slow and looked forward to seeing them each year. They finally sold the business after she passed away from cancer. The show was especially good for us as we could stay with friends, thereby saving money. On the Saturday before the end of the show, we said goodbye to Mike and Mitch as they jumped into the Honda on their way to Florida. They would spend the Ball State spring break with

Mitch's sister, Lisa, in Palmetto, Florida. A happy couple. When the show finished, we celebrated with everyone, satisfied that it had been a successful investment in advertising dollars. A snowstorm was coming, so we left early in the morning for Illinois. We stopped in a small town with one of our customers from last year. They owned a farm, and we picked up half a cow that they had prepared for us. After an overnight stay in Eau Claire, Wisconsin, we got home safely. Happy to be home.

A good day's catch

Our first catch

A view down the lake

Our home and office

Son Jim, Dec '81, Cabin #3

Original interior – Cabin #2

Aerial Photo of our resort

Netting the "Big One"

Front cover of brochure, photo by Jim

Advertising

Jerry and Joann celebrating Jerry's birthday

"What Have We Done?"

Kathie's father, Al, in his workshop

Our "best selling" T-Shirt

PART 3: MIKE

The Call

On our second day home, the phone rang, and it was Mitch calling from Florida. She told us that Mike had been hospitalized the night before after suffering stroke-like symptoms while they were eating dinner. No one knew the cause of his problem, but he was scheduled for a CAT scan later that day.

One phone call and our lives were turned upside down. We had to go to Florida. Jim was still in school, and we needed to know what was happening to Mike. What to do? Who to call? So many decisions - so little time. After much discussion, we decided that Kathie should immediately fly to Florida. Jim had been planning to spend his spring break in Indianapolis with Lisa so we decided that he and I would drive to Indianapolis and then I would fly from there to Florida. When Mitch called, she said she was having many difficulties finding out what the hospital was doing as she was not a relative and of course, Mike didn't have a family doctor in Florida. I remembered that an old friend from our time in Ethiopia. Doctor Carl Graves, was in private practice in Dade City, Florida, which was near Palmetto. I was able to reach Carl and asked him to act as our family doctor, thus cutting through the hospital red tape. Jim and I left shortly thereafter. Kathie stayed behind as her flight didn't leave until the following morning. Carl jumped on the problem and called Kathie, saying that it appeared from the CAT Scan that Mike's symptoms were caused by a large aneurysm in his brain and that surgery would be needed. I called Kathie while we were driving south, and she filled me in on what Carl had told her. Denny's wife, Connie, took Kathie to Duluth the next morning.

Jim stayed in Indianapolis with his girlfriend Lisa, and I flew on to Florida. We all met at the Manatee Memorial Hospital in Bradenton where Mike was hospitalized. We met with the neurosurgeon who explained that the aneurysm was located on the Basilar artery deep within Mike's brain. It was explained that if you drew a line from your forehead to the back of your head and another between your ears, the Basilar artery was where the lines intersected. He said that the aneurysm was most likely congenital and that this sort of thing would manifest itself in a person's late teens or early 20s. Mike was 20. He was confident that the aneurysm could be repaired without significant impact on Mike's future. Mike was also very fortunate to have suffered the symptoms without the aneurysm breaking as that would have certainly killed him.

Carl had joined us and told us that the neurosurgeon's reputation was excellent as we knew nothing of his medical qualifications. Mike had recovered from his attack, and together we all agreed on the surgery, and it was scheduled for the next day. We called Jim and scheduled a flight for him to arrive after the surgery was completed. Friends of our old neighbors in Indianapolis, Molly, and Don Barr, offered us a place to stay. When we got to their place, it was obvious they never expected us to say "Yes" but at the time we had few options. We made the couple that we were staying with extremely happy when we moved out. We will always remember the sign they had hanging in their kitchen: "Fish and Guests Stink after three days". They lived by that motto, but we did appreciate them tolerating us in their home those first few days.

The next day we all gathered at the hospital and said our "brave" best wishes to Mike as he was wheeled into surgery. What a feeling! The surgeon had told us that the procedure would take about three hours, so we settled in for a long wait.

The Outside View

I had been writing a weekly column under the pseudonym "the Perch" for the *Ely Miner* and as the wait began, I settled in and wrote the following column:

"I am writing this column sitting on the banks of the Manatee River in Bradenton, Florida, as my son undergoes his surgery in a hospital some five hundred yards away. As with my last column, hope and fear continue to do battle. The days since our arrival have meshed together into one continuous period of tests, discussions with doctors, and large periods of encouraging words with our son.

As he departed for surgery, a feeling of relief, coupled with fear, settled over me. Relief that our chance to correct his problem had finally arrived, and fear as to the potential negative results which could occur. Our hopes have been strengthened by my sources. Primarily from our son, who through participation with the Student Life and Campus Crusade programs in high school and college had come to know and trust his God. His inner calm and strength support us all. Additionally, he had attended a local church while on vacation and the pastor and congregation has adopted us in these trying times.

We are also lucky to have personal friends in the local

area who have helped us with lodging, etc., etc. This total togetherness of family, old friends, and many new friends, gives us all the strength to continue.

It will still be a few hours before the true results of the operation are known and as I finish this column, I am overcome with hope and a realization that no matter what the outcome, we will continue together as a family and overcome this problem. So, hug your children and kiss your husband or wife, and count the blessings that God has given you as a family.

Smile,

The "Perch."

Surgery

Surgery started in mid-morning, and after more than four hours passed without a word, panic slowly began to set in. Fear took command, and as the minutes and hours dragged on, we came close to a frenzy. Finally, we got word that Mike was in recovery but nothing from the doctor. Then a message, again not directly from the surgeon, that the surgery had not gone well, and the surgeon had left the hospital. The pastor from Lisa's church called the surgeon's office, and I was able to talk briefly with Dr. Barnes. He explained the rupture of the aneurysm. I asked about recovery and problems ahead and got a vague answer about double vision. I called Dr. Graves in Dade City who promised to contact Barnes for more information. It is difficult to express the sheer terror of not knowing what was happening particularly immediately following the surgery. Only on TV does the surgeon appear, wiping his hands, to brief everyone on the patient's prognosis. The point here is to emphasize the need for a strong support group. Kathie and I, while still under control, could not function well in terms of calling Dr. Barnes, etc. This is where the pastor and Doc Graves came to our rescue.

Difficulties had indeed been encountered. The aneurysm had not been the easily corrected "bubble" envisioned prior to the surgery. Instead, because it had been present for such a long time, it had filtered into the creases in the brain and looked more like a spider web than a bubble. As the artery was "clipped" to remove the aneurysm, it had dissolved. This, in effect, had created a stroke as the normal blood flow through the artery had been interrupted. This interruption had caused an "insult" to parts of the brain that needed this blood flow to sustain normal functions. The rupture had been repaired but the surgeon had no idea as to what would result in brain function due to the insult. He felt the next 24 - 48 hours would be critical in determining the outcome. We were stunned because prior to surgery we had been told that after a brief period of hospitalization, Mike would be able to resume a normal life. As time passed, we would grow to hate the word, "normal."

We saw Mike in intensive care afterward. Here was a 265-pound college football player, hooked up to every device available. His head and face looked to be twice its normal size, and he was in a deep coma. Later that evening, we talked with one doctor about donating his organs should he not survive the night. His response was "He'd be a great donor due to his age and physical condition." Sleep that night was impossible as we came to grips with the fact that we were facing a long-term situation in a strange town, 2,000 miles from home.

In later years, people have asked many times, "How did you ever do it?" In my mind the answer was simple, we just did what we had to do. But, of course, things were not that simple. One major help was the instant support we received from those around us. We had called Jerry and JoAnn from Florida, and suddenly there they were at the hospital. When they had heard what was happening, they'd dropped everything and drove from El Paso, Texas to be with us. Jim was with us as well as Mitch and her sister. The pastor of Lisa's church and the congregation immediately offered their support and assistance.

The next day Mike was still with us and was moved into an intensive care ward. From the nurses we found out that the surgeon hoped that Mike would regain consciousness and begin to talk shortly. He did emerge from the coma but did not speak.

Knowing that our stay in Florida would be long, Carl Graves came to our rescue by offering us the use of his motor home to stay in. Lisa had a small apartment in a private home. The home, owned by a wonderful elderly couple, the Greens, had a large, wide driveway. The Greens offered to allow us to park the motor home there, and Lisa offered the use of her bathroom. We had "living" accommodations. Carl also prescribed some sleeping medication for us as he could tell the toll things were beginning to take on us.

We shared a great deal with Lisa. We shared meals, bathrooms, and dreams for over two months. She was about 24, and very active in the Bradenton Brethren Church. After the surgery, she literally allowed her life to be completely altered for those months. She became a full member of Mike's support team, visiting him nearly every day in the hospital after work. Kathie and I would look forward to her bounce and bright smile each day. We shared her downs when Mike would greet her with tears and her ups when she shared positive events with us. To us, she was a prime example of people stepping forward in a time of need. It's a rare quality and one which should be appreciated and cherished. Her support was a clear demonstration of how God wants everyone to treat their fellow man.

In those first few days, Mike showed very little visible signs of improvement. Mitch had to return to school. Before she left, she made one rather stark comment that we've never forgotten. She told us that "her Mike had died on the operating table." It was stunning, blunt and, as time would tell, true. We also decided that Jim would return home to continue to keep the home fires burning and return to school. This put him into a most difficult situation which I'll write about later. Jerry and JoAnn also returned to their home, but their instant support will always be remembered.

Our days were spent at the hospital. Mike slowly became more alert but remained non-verbal. We felt that he was making progress. I could get him to squeeze my hand in response to questions and began to have the feeling that he was aware of his surroundings. I often said he was like the "genie in a bottle," waiting for someone to pull the cork. He could make sounds but said no words. Feeding him was very difficult in that he was like a 2-month-old. We'd put food in his mouth only to see his tongue push most of it out onto his bib. One good thing was that he was "loved" by all his nurses. Here was this handsome 20-year-old football player to care for. Much better than the elderly, sometimes crabby, elderly patients they normally worked with.

Mike's lack of progress in talking was causing concern. At one point, Carl even suggested to me that his future looked so bleak that we should consider applying for Social Security as most likely, he would spend the rest of his days confined to a nursing home. The nurses said the surgeon was frustrated but he did order a speech therapist to work with Mike. Enter Pat Flemming. We had just finished feeding Mike lunch when Pat arrived. She saw the trouble he was having with the meal. After we'd talked for a while, she asked us to leave her alone with Mike that afternoon as she felt he would respond better without us watching his every move.

When we returned to feed him supper, there was a miracle waiting for us. Mike was able to slowly eat without dribbling most of the food onto himself. Pat was beaming. When we asked her how this could happen, she offered the following explanation, something which I have never forgotten. Pat had asked Mike to concentrate on swallowing. She told him that as you swallow, your tongue "automatically" goes to the roof of your mouth and drags the food down your throat. In Mike's case he had to concentrate on moving his tongue to the roof of his mouth and train himself to swallow properly. What a wonderful sight. We left that evening on a real "high."

Speaking of high's. Each day was filled with either highs or lows. If we felt Mike was improving, a high. If he had a difficult day, a low. Both Kathie and I suffered the same high's and ow's. Somehow when one was Low, the other was there to help overcome the Low. Carl and Pat had shared many stories of how a situation like Mike's had broken apart many families. Everyone was frustrated with the "cards they'd been dealt."

I do not believe that words will ever be able to describe the pain of the events immediately prior to and after the surgery. There was a sense of total helplessness coupled with a fear that I had never experienced. It was at this point that the idea of being totally independent crumbles. Such a circumstance literally forces one to become totally dependent upon loved ones, and whatever friends are willing to step forward to help. First and foremost was Kathie; without her, everything would have been impossible. While our personal needs were not openly discussed during the months in Florida, we became totally dependent upon each other to maintain our emotional balance. However, there were times that we found ourselves shouting at each other in the car over things which turned out to be totally insignificant. One really begins to believe the saying "that you only hurt the one you love." Somehow over time, we were able to struggle through these periods. I don't believe either one of us realized the significance of this dependence until much later.

After each visit with Mike at Manatee and later Blake, we compared mental notes about what we thought we saw in terms of progress. A stronger handshake, more recognition or awareness of his surroundings, etc. There were many times, particularly before Mike began to talk, that I would stand in the hallway at Manatee in front of a window looking at the river and attempt to talk with God. You need to know that these "discussions" had been few and far between for me and I really don't know if they were successful. I felt somewhat hypocritical turning to God when things are bad while generally ignoring him when things are good. However, I do believe that God is there to listen and support in times of need.

Somehow after these discussions and some tears, I had the strength to return to Mike's bedside with an up feeling. Kathie told me she'd prayed to God that first night in intensive care to let us have our boy no matter what the outcome of the surgery. The Pastor from Lisa's church also continued to provide us strong support and his congregation welcomed us at Sunday services. I firmly believe that Mike's acceptance of Jesus through his high school and his college Campus Life experiences were now helping him cope with his circumstances. Further evidence of this happened shortly thereafter.

One day, Mike Mathioudakis came to the hospital. Mike and our Mike had played football in high school together and Mike was attending Notre Dame University. He was in Sarasota on spring break working on a project for Campus Life. His visit sparked the first words from Mike. What a wonderful day. I think God was in the room with them during that visit. Mike added words each day and everyone on the staff knew that progress was being made, with one exception.

The nurses told us that our surgeon was totally discouraged by Mike's failure to talk. He would come into intensive care, not visit Mike, and simply write "No Progress" on his chart and leave. Finally, they got him to visit Mike and Mike said, "Hello Doc." What a day! The surgeon immediately called us in and recommended that Mike be transferred to Blake Rehabilitation Hospital in Bradenton. Mike was moved the next day. It was now early April 1984.

Blake Rehabilitation Hospital

Blake was a totally different hospital environment. Mike had daily work with speech, physical, and occupational therapy. Pat did not work at Blake, so she wasn't directly involved with his therapy. We are still in contact with her; what a wonderful woman. The challenge for Mike was enormous as he basically had to learn to walk, talk, and think all over again. Because of his work schedule, we would normally only visit in the evenings or periodically to watch as he struggled during his sessions. Throughout Mike's therapy, he used many ingenious devices to redevelop his muscles, speech, coordination, and general alertness. These ran the gauntlet from sucking ice to strengthen his throat muscles to various games to improve eye and hand coordination, to Pac-Man. To me, it was amazing to witness the innovative approaches used by the various therapists. His problems were somewhat like those encountered by a stroke victim, i.e., right-side paralysis, inability to walk, weakness in the small motor muscles of his hands, and numerous problems with his speech.

Major events included escaping from a wheelchair to the sticks, the ability to hold a pencil in his right hand, and he began to write again. Being able to catch a ball and of course, Pac-Man. Blake had received one machine as a gift, and shortly before his discharge, Mike was encouraged to play all comers. Again, an innocent event; however, the eye-hand coordination needed to play the game was an invaluable assist to his recovery. We learned that due to cognitive problems, he would interpret things literally. At one session, he was asked the meaning of "strike when the iron was hot." His response was "hit someone with a hot iron." This literal interpretation of thoughts and ideas would cause many difficulties between us in the future. I tend to be sarcastic, and when Mike would interpret my comments literally, it would create these problems.

While all of this was going on, Carl sold the motor home we were living in but promptly appeared with a trailer that he had procured to replace the motor home. Carl also insisted that we leave Mike and visit him and his family periodically. While it was difficult to leave, these breaks were important to our sanity, and I'm sure good for Mike to be on his own.

We were constantly thinking about the resort and how we were going to manage it. The Chamber of Commerce had been forwarding us prospect lists, so we were able to mail out our brochures, and we were getting reservations while in Florida. Jim called us one day to announce that he'd dropped out of Vermilion Community College. He'd decided that he just couldn't concentrate on his studies with all that was happening. Fortunately, he had grown close to Denny and his family, which offered him a place to go to escape the loneliness of a cold Minnesota winter. Jim told us that he and Denny were finishing the project in the basement, getting it ready to become our new office/store for the new season.

Mike was now able to walk with the assistance of two canes, that he called "sticks". Easter Sunday was approaching, and we asked the hospital for permission to take him to Easter services at Lisa's church. About a week before Easter, Mike was granted his first pass from Blake, and we spent the afternoon swimming at my sister-in-law's mother's mobile home park. We finished the day having dinner with Lisa at Mrs. Green's. When it was time to take Mike back to the hospital things changed dramatically.

Mike had decided that he was "normal" and there was no need to return to the hospital. All along he had had difficulty expressing himself and would periodically cry uncontrollably. He started to do this as we drove to the hospital. By the time we got on the elevator and started for his floor, the crying had turned into a very loud howl. You can imagine what noise a 6'5", 265 pound man could make. When the doors to the elevator opened, it was all we could do to get a nurse to handle him, and we literally fled the scene. We could hear his howl all the way down the elevator, our hearts broken. The next day he was so upset that a full day of therapy was lost. Future passes would not be granted until he regained control.

This is a good point to discuss "lability." Its definition is: "The unregulated or unstable state of emotions or mood, characterized by exaggerated, affective expression." It's a medical term that, to us, meant crying, while to the doctors, it is a type of release for an individual who has no other way to express themselves. Mike used this form of release for a long time. The crying came at any time and for any reason, and for reasons we and he will probably never understand. When it happened over the years, we would relate it to distress, unhappiness, and probably embarrassment because I am sure there were times when he did not know why he was crying. Fortunately, when Easter arrived, he had regained control, and the pass was granted.

While I'm no expert on the Bible, my interpretation of Easter is "rebirth," and that day constituted Mike's rebirth as an individual. As you might expect, we were extremely apprehensive, not knowing how he would react because of our earlier problems. Church was at the Bradenton Brethren Church which, due to Lisa's association, had "adopted" us. Church members were aware of his plight and welcomed him with open arms, which made the next three hours a true "high" in Mike's struggle back. During the service, he insisted on standing for the hymns on his sticks and even attempted to sing along with the congregation. There were many tears that day, and I believe we all left knowing that God was with us all and that he had many more plans for Mike.

As we approached the end of April, it became apparent that Blake had done all it could for Mike. He still was not out of the woods and needed additional speech, physical, and especially cognitive help. After discussions with the doctors, we decided that he may be able to do better in more familiar surroundings, so we decided to move him to Indianapolis. Our thought was that he'd be near his girlfriend Mitch, other college friends, plus Indianapolis had well-known rehabilitation facilities. Our Florida doctors referred us to a Dr. White who worked for the Hook Rehabilitation Center.

Return to Indianapolis

We decided that Kathie and Mike would fly to Indy while I drove the Honda back. Jim would meet us in Indianapolis. During their flight, Kathie discovered that Mike was suffering from another problem. He had lost his gag reflex. While they were changing planes in Atlanta, Mike was eating a hot dog and started choking. Somehow, Kathie was able to get the piece of meat dislodged, but that problem still plagues Mike today.

The Mathiedokis' had agreed to let us stay temporarily with them while we found longer-term housing. Mike was happy to be among friends but was resisting the idea that he needed additional therapy. When he was evaluated by Dr. White, it was determined that his needs were more specialized than what Hook could provide, and we were referred to a place named the Indianapolis Center for Neurological Rehabilitation (CNR).

Center for Neurological Rehabilitation (CNR)

In 1984, CNR was one of the few facilities in the United States which dealt with the cognitive reasoning problems Mike faced. The program that Mike entered was an outpatient situation consisting of five days a week. It was apparent that it could take the entire summer. The emphasis would be upon improving his cognitive ability. From a parent's point of view, CNR offered a good example of the problems one faces when seeking help for a brain-damaged person. We knew Mike needed help after his release from Blake but found it frustrating when we attempted to locate a facility. While we think CNR helped Mike somewhat, we'll never know. You are placed in a situation, depending on a "for-profit" organization costing $150 per day, dealing with your son's brain. Also, because such therapy was "new," it was not covered by insurance. Despite all of this, we felt we had little choice but to proceed. Kathie and I started looking at apartments, and it soon became apparent that between the cost of the Center and housing, we were in for a long, lean summer. Suddenly our old Army friends, Nev and Jane Holder, came to our rescue. Their house had a "mother-in-law" apartment, and they offered its use to Kathie and Mike. What a lifesaver. A nice place to live plus being with good friends. Great support for Mike and especially Kathie.

Our plan was for Jim and me to operate the resort while Kathie and Mike remained in Indianapolis. It would mean a long summer for everyone but something that had to be done. Kathie would take Mike to the Center each morning, and to save her sanity, she decided to seek work. Before we retired, she had worked for a Hickory Farms store in a local mall, and they agreed to hire her for the summer. Mike was not at all happy with the Center, so Kathie had her hands full between his objections and our separation. She faced many difficult situations as the days and weeks rolled by.

Northern Lights Lodge

While this was going on, Jim and I did our best to keep the resort operating. Not being the best house cleaners, we hired a local lady to come in each Saturday morning to help us clean cabins. This worked well, and we were able to keep our heads above water that summer. Compared to Kathie, my responsibilities and loneliness were simple. I did learn that a woman was important for the business, as I found myself unable to respond to questions from our female guests the way Kathie could.

The Dogs

During the summer, we lost our dachshund Max, who somehow ran under the wheels of our truck when Jim was taking garbage to the dump. Before that happened, the dogs had gotten into a skunk one day. We'd been burying the fish guts from our fish cleaning house rather than taking them to the dump. Apparently, this is what attracted the skunk, and one day the three dogs went flying into the woods barking like crazy. When I went to investigate, there was a skunk. I yelled and ran as did the dachshunds, but Bob had to stay and investigate. His reward was a snoot full of spray. Wow, what a smell. Our first step was to throw him into the lake. The wrong move as the water just made the smell worse. We then tried tomato juice, but it didn't work, and we didn't have enough juice. Finally, I called the vet who had some stuff called "Skunk Off." It worked the best but for the rest of the summer whenever Bob went to the beach for a swim, he would come out of the water smelling like a skunk. Quite a lesson.

When we could, Jim and I would sneak off for an hour or so to fish down the river. The trips usually lasted for an hour or two in the evening. On many occasions, we'd return to find Ralf sitting outside and the house messed up by the three dogs. All would be disciplined. Later we discovered that Ralf had learned to jump from the bed in the spare bedroom to the chest of drawers and then push out the screen. He then jumped out of the window. He suffered from separation anxiety which would become an issue later.

Return to Ely

Kathie was having lots of problems with both Mike and the Center. Mike didn't want to be there, saying all along that he was back to normal – that word again. The staff of the Center were equally frustrated in what they saw as a lack of progress on his part. Kathie had hoped to celebrate Mike's 21st birthday at the Center but was basically ignored by the staff and finally, towards the beginning of August, we made the decision to have Mike withdraw from the Center.

Mike insisted that he would be able to return to school in September, so we completed arrangements for him to enroll. Kathie and Mike then returned to the resort in early August. Before leaving the Center, she was advised by the staff that Mike would only "crash and burn" in college and to return him once that had happened.

They were both extremely happy to be home. Mike continued to insist that he was "normal," but his actions around the resort indicated that he still had a long way to go. We were painting the garage one day and he'd stuck the brush as well as half of his hand into the paint bucket and then become very upset with himself. Early on, Pat Flemming had told us about patients with brain injuries progressing through "plateaus" and that it was important to keep them from becoming satisfied at their current plateau because if they did, progress towards full recovery would become extremely difficult. We are still working on these plateaus.

At the same time, bills for Mike's surgery, therapy, etc., continued to flow in. By pure luck, since he was in college and under 21 when everything happened, my military insurance, CHAMPUS, covered some of the expenses, maybe 50 percent of those items covered. The State of Indiana had also picked up part of the $150 per day charges at the Center, but as things began to settle out, we knew we were facing significant debts. My first painful decision was to tell Jim that there would be no way in the near future that we could pay for his college education. I then started looking for work during the off-season. Somehow, we needed to make money during those six months.

By the time Mike and Kathie returned, Jim was very frustrated. He had basically been the odd man out for the previous six months as all our attention was directed towards Mike. While we were gone, he and

Denny had done a great job redoing the garage and making it into an office/small store. Paneling was up, and they even put in a false drop ceiling. It was bright and welcoming for our guests. He had also bought his first car that summer. He and I had worked together well while the others were gone, but he decided that the last thing he wanted was to spend another lonely winter in Minnesota. In late August, he packed up and left for Indianapolis. Shortly after he arrived, he called to tell us he'd gotten a job on the grounds crew of a local golf course.

After Labor Day, we put Mike on a plane for Indianapolis for his return to Ball State. His scholarship was still in effect, so he had room, board and tuition taken care of by the school. Kathie will never forget watching him cry as he boarded the plane. Crying was one way for him to release his frustrations and concerns.

My search for work was not going well as folks weren't terribly interested once I told them I wanted a good paying job for only six months. Again, I firmly believe that the hand of God entered the picture, not for my sake, but for Mike. Our friends, the Holders called and told me that another Army friend, Ron Carlson, was working for a firm that had a contract to work with the Finance Center on an accounting problem. Ron was looking for help, and he had asked that I call him. I called, explained my circumstances, and he hired me over the phone with a start date in mid-October. Our prayers were answered.

The rest of September and early October were spent working on getting the resort closed for the winter once our last summer guest had departed. No matter what, we had to shut down in late September, as once the weather turned cold, the water lines to the cabins were subject to freezing. Kathie worked on trying to find us a place to live. We hit dead ends a couple of times when we told them we had two dogs, and one was over 50 pounds. Finally, one place agreed to rent us a two-bedroom townhouse near Fort Harrison where I would be working. We had decided to rent a trailer and take a bed, couch, table, etc., with us to the apartment. About a week before leaving, I reserved a 6x12 foot covered trailer from the U-Haul place in Virginia. The day I arrived to pick it up, I discovered it had been rented to someone else. This was particularly bad as the area's iron ore mine had closed and demand for trailers was high as people were forced to relocate to find work. I drove to Duluth/Superior, Wisconsin, looking for a trailer without success. However, they were able to find me one in Grand Rapids about 100 miles away. It took all day and nearly 300 miles of driving, but we had our trailer. Finally, we headed south to a new temporary home and a new job.

Our Return to Indianapolis

Prior to leaving, we had asked Jim if he would like to live with us that winter. It would save him rent money, plus he'd be able to enjoy his mom's cooking. He readily agreed and met us at the apartment and helped us unload the trailer, return it, and set up furniture, etc. When everything was completed, we decided to go to dinner, Jim's treat. We left Ralf in one bedroom and Bob in the other bedroom. Afterwards, we returned to find Bob asleep on the bed and Ralf in a frenzy. In front of the bedroom door, he'd dug out a semicircle of the shag carpet. In the apartment less than six hours and already damage. The next morning before leaving for the commissary to buy food, we left Bob in the bedroom and decided to put Ralf in the bathroom thinking that with the tile floor he'd be unable to get into more mischief. Wrong! When we returned, Bob was asleep on the bed and Ralf had ripped a big piece of molding out from around the bathroom door. That weekend, Kathie drove to Cleveland to visit her mom. Ralf went with her, and Hilda was thrilled when Kathie offered to let her keep him. They became great companions until Hilda's death years later. Ralf limited his problems because Hilda was almost always at home with him.

The winter went reasonably well. Kathie worked again at Hickory Farms, and my job was interesting. As I was working for a government contractor, I was able to receive my full salary, which made the winter a success. We were able to keep current with Mike's medical bills and save enough money to make sure we'd be able to make the payment for the extra land. Business for the resort was continuing to improve, and of course, we were able to work the Sport Show in February.

Ball State University

Mike almost immediately encountered problems at Ball State. When he was hospitalized, he had received several get-well cards, etc., from his fellow students. He chose to return to the dorm he had been in prior to his problems. It soon became evident that this had been the wrong decision. Simply put, the Mike that had left for spring break that March was not the Mike that returned to school in September. The "new" Mike had difficulty talking, he walked with a limp, and it took him time to formulate what he wanted to say. The "old" Mike was the big football player, life of the party, very articulate and popular. Unfortunately, his fellow students for the most part reacted to him the way they reacted to others with disabilities; they either ignored or avoided him. He suddenly was facing silent discrimination which significantly hurt his fragile self-confidence. He also discovered that his course material was much more difficult than it had been. On many occasions, he would call, and we would hop into the car and drive to Ball State in Muncie, IN, some 45 miles north of Indianapolis to help him get himself and the situations he was facing under control. It was these visits that made me understand why God had opened the door for my job.

Towards the end of that first semester, we received a call from his counselor. We met and found out that Mike was on the verge of failing his coursework. If he continued, the failures counted against his grade point average would place his academic standing in jeopardy. She recommended that we change his status to "audit," which would eliminate grades for that term and change his major from math/computer science to undecided. This would allow him to select somewhat easier coursework for the coming semester. The counselor also shared with us that she too had suffered an aneurysm as a young adult and had complete empathy for Mike's situation. God's hand was on his shoulder again.

We also had a long conversation with Mike's football coach. He was not the head coach that had recruited Mike, so we were concerned about his attitude towards Mike as he was using a scholarship without being able to contribute to the football program. The coach suggested that Mike may want a different environment to continue his college career. Mike replied that he wanted to remain at Ball State. The coach then shared with us that his college-age daughter had recently been in a serious automobile accident and suffered a significant brain injury. His move from the University of Michigan to Ball State had seemed to help in her recovery. He had complete empathy for Mike and on the spot agreed to honor his full scholarship. This was significant as the coach was releasing a full scholarship for the next 3-plus years. God's hand was on Mike's shoulder again.

As the new semester started, Mike returned to his studies with renewed interest. Just maybe he had been able to climb to another plateau. The University also provided speech therapy for him. Ball State had an excellent school specializing in training students in speech therapy, so it was a perfect fit for him. In a final step, Mike changed dorms. He moved into a smaller dorm where none of the students had known him before his surgery. There the students accepted him for who he was, not what he had been.

Toward the end of April, the business I was working for lost the government contract. It was my first experience with "public" firings as our supervisor would walk out of his office, go to a person's desk, and tell them they were out and pack up and leave. Having never worked in this environment, it was quite an education. As I was about to leave anyway, I was never fired but it did tell me that a similar opportunity would not be available for the coming October. I had to find something else.

PART 4: OUR RETURN HOME

Our Return

Jim opted to remain in Indianapolis and work, and we helped him move into a rented room prior to heading out for the resort. We were not happy with his living environment but knew it had to be his decision. Later, he would call and tell us he'd enrolled in night classes in Law Enforcement at a local university. We were very happy with that news.

The summer at the resort went well. Mike was getting better each day and started to contribute to the operation. He also became close with Audie and Carol Austreng and began attending church with them on a regular basis. Our weeks ran Saturday afternoon through Saturday morning, which made Sunday an important day. Working with our new guests and

Kathie and I never took the opportunity to accompany Mike to church. Later that year, he chose to be "re-baptized," which was done one Sunday in Birch Lake. The baptism was an event I'll never forget. He, Audie, and Carol were all baptized in the lake. Prior to the event, each presented a testimony, and Mike re-living his ordeal coupled with his thanks for the support he received caused no one to leave with a dry eye. As the summer progressed, we also grew closer to the Austrengs, having them out for our weekly resort cookouts, etc. I was still writing my column for the Babbitt Weekly News, and in the middle of August, I got Mike to write a small piece for my column.

Outside View

"I am most pleased to introduce a 'guest columnist' this week. For those of you who have followed through our family experiences, you know this new writer – our son. To help him through his therapy, I have asked him to recount his own thoughts during his recuperation. His column follows:

'I've been able to come home after a five-month battle with my aneurysm in my brain. I am still battling the problem with my voice. Prayerfully, it will return to normal. The last five months have been a battle each day. I remember when it took five people for me to walk. Be proud you live and work in a beautiful part of this country. I've come a long way in a short time, but I still have a little way to go. I'm so proud to have a beautiful family behind me! Thank you so much.'

To my readers, I say thanks for allowing me to share this small piece of personal feelings with you. Again, I urge you to cherish what you have and not be afraid to work to protect what you have. Hug your kids for me.

Smile,

The 'Perch."

The River

Audie also was interested in investigating the possibility of conducting guided raft trips down the Roaring Stoney River. It was a beautiful section of river, about three miles long. The route would be from the bridge on dirt road called the Tomahawk Trail to Birch Lake. He decided that he would do the float one day when the water was running good and asked Mike to join him. It turned out to be a wild ride with both Mike and Audie being ejected from the rafts, being caught in the swift current, etc. Both made it ok, quite wet, and very tired. Looking back, it's a miracle that Mike wasn't hurt as his coordination was still on the mend. We talked at great length about trying to promote these trips for next summer. However, we never did act on that idea. This turned out to be a good decision as in the coming years water levels on the river were very low and would not have allowed us to do the trips. Later we learned where to fish on the Roaring Stoney River and caught several large Northern Pike using our canoe.

In addition to the river idea, Audie was always a visionary. He helped develop a large building in Babbitt into a business center, and I admired him for his efforts to bring business into the community. We even visited other communities with the idea of offering our assistance to help them promote their areas. Unfortunately, this idea was not well received. Later, Audie would suffer a stroke after complications from heart surgery. The stroke left him unable to talk, and while remaining close friends, our business ideas ceased.

Bob

Bob was now our "full-time resort dog." He thrived at the resort, roaming free throughout the resort. Later, we also discovered that he would visit our neighbor resort and their dog, Boo Boo, on a regular basis. He was good and normally came running when his name was called. If we had to look for him, we would usually find him next door. The kids staying at the resort loved him and would knock on the door to ask if Bob could come out to play. He and the kids would spend hours on the beach playing with the frisbee. The boys and girls also loved to bring him plates of leftover food. One day a little girl brought him her plate. He cleaned off everything except for the peas. She studied the plate and said, "that's OK Bob, I didn't like them either." What a laugh. It's a wonder how you remember those little things. He also became a star at our weekly cookouts. Patiently waiting his turn and refraining from begging, he would get his reward when I handed him his own hamburger, bun, and all. He would carry it into the woods and eat it in peace. Over the years, whenever we needed a laugh, Bob would provide it. In his later years, we discovered that each morning, he would visit each cabin. Sit on the steps, make a couple of small woofs, and await his breakfast. Some guests would cook him a full breakfast! We also created a T-shirt with his photo and the words, "I met Bob at Northern Lights Lodge." It was, by far, our bestselling shirt over the years.

Septic Systems

Our septic systems were always a problem. Each cabin and the house had its own septic system. Unfortunately, they had been installed in the 50s when the resort was built and were very small, only 250 gallons. The "gray water" from the sinks was piped into 55-gallon drums buried beneath the cabin. By the 1980s, rules on septic had changed considerably. The old tanks simply had a few feet of pipe buried in the ground for the overflow instead of the specially built "drain" fields now required. My nose has never been sensitive, but I soon learned how to smell the "sweet" ooze of a full septic tank. In those first years, we redid the tanks and drain fields for Cabins 3, 4, and 5. The other cabins plus the house also needed similar work. We were lucky that the resort was built on a gravel hillside which provided a natural drain field. Many other resorts in the area were built on ledge rock which required building special and expensive mound systems for the drain fields. As we entered the 90s, regulations for septic systems became an even larger issue as State laws were changing almost every year.

The Ely Miner

Fall was rapidly approaching, and Mike prepared to go back to school. I was still without winter work, and prospects looked dim. One day Audie approached me and asked if I would be interested in working as Editor for the Ely Miner that winter. His daughter and son-in-law had been running the newspaper, but the son-in-law had accepted another newspaper job in Grand Rapids which would pay more and help them raise their family. With no other prospects, I accepted. My pay would be $600 per month.

The Job

The Ely Miner was a weekly newspaper printed on Friday. In addition to myself, there was one other employee, Penny Popish. She was the secretary, typesetter, and "jack of all trades." The office was open for normal business each day of the week. My job was to sell advertising, organize the paper, collect articles, and write articles and editorials. One of the first things I did was to review the accounts. It was clear that the paper was losing money each month.

Our three sources of income — advertising, subscriptions, and printing a monthly newspaper for the Yugoslav Club — were not keeping pace with our expenses. Our printing was done by a newspaper in Virginia, MN. They were carrying the expense of printing, which was the only reason we were still in business. Competition for advertising dollars in Ely was extreme, as there was another weekly newspaper, *The Ely Echo*, and a weekly Shopper. Ely was a summer town, and businesses in town were very slow in the winter, making owners very reluctant to spend lots of dollars on advertising. Selling ads was the most difficult part of the job. Being in business myself, I could understand the owner's reluctance to buy ads. I found that I was not good at pushing folks to buy ads and, quite frankly, I hated that part of the job.

On the other hand, creating a newspaper was very interesting and exciting. Each week, we would start from scratch. For the most part, the local news consisted of reporting on City Council meetings, school board meetings, and maybe a police report. Covering these events was very time-consuming, and I soon discovered that my monthly salary of $600 represented about $1.00 per hour. I tried to write editorials which made sense and addressed subjects of interest. In a small town that was not busy in the winter, small stories could "grow" into big ones through rumor. I tried to at least get the facts as correct as possible. I was also the primary photographer for the paper and, on occasion, would pick a topic and do interviews on the street concerning that week's topic. I also continued to write my column for the Babbitt paper. I learned from attending meetings that I was and would always be an "outsider" in the community. In Ely, if you were not a graduate of Ely High School, you were tolerated but never really included.

The Miner was more than 100 years old, and I discovered that copies of the old newspapers were in a safe in City Hall. They were great reading, and I tried to include at least one article from back in the 20s or 30s in each edition. Ely was a wild town back then. Lots of lumberjacks, women of ill repute, and even gunfights. No one worried about being sued back then, as folks were commonly referred to as no-good scoundrels!

Kathie soon became an "unpaid" part of the staff. She proved to be an excellent proofreader. She and Carol would also take weekly trips to Virginia, MN, selling ads. It was most difficult for Kathie as Carol was a very intense person, and when Kathie sold an ad, Carol would complain that the ad wasn't big enough. I'll never know how Kathie put up with this.

Thursday evening was our "big" time. Throughout the week, my articles, ads, etc., were typed by Penny on a wax type of paper. Photos were also developed and transferred to the same type of paper. After work, Kathie and I, plus Audie and Carol, would meet in the Babbitt Weekly office and literally put together the two newspapers. Each page, about 24 inches wide and 36 inches tall, would be created by sticking waxed paper articles onto the pages. Photos were placed, columns established, and the page slowly created. Audie was very good at laying out the pages, and I learned a great deal from him. While we were working on this, Carol and Kathie would put together the "shopper" portion of the paper. Proofreading of the ads was critical as a mistake would create many unwanted problems with the advertiser. The papers were Audie and Carol's only source of income, so the evening could become very intense as the papers were created. Usually, we were able to finish between 8 and 9 p.m. and would reward ourselves by stopping and having dinner at a local bar before heading home.

It was my job to have the newspapers printed the following morning. This was also quite a project, especially once our deep winter had settled in. Audie owned a little Toyota pickup truck that I used. It was a bucket of rust, and I could see through the floorboard as I drove the truck. Our paper had to be at the Virginia printing plant by 5 a.m. Therefore, I'd leave at 4 a.m. each Friday. On a typical morning from mid-December until mid-March, the temperature when I left was somewhere between -25 and -30. To make sure the truck would start I would park it in the neighboring resort's garage as we had no garage. Somehow, it would always start, and off I'd go. Fortunately, it rarely snowed when it was that cold, so I would only have to worry about ice and the cold wind blowing through the floorboards!

When I got to the plant, the printing operation was very interesting. Each page would be photographed, and I would proof the negatives, ensuring that all the clear spots were filled in with pencil. As it was a negative, clear spots would print black if they were not filled in. The negatives would then be used to produce tin printing plates, which would then be placed on the rollers of the press. Soon, the press would roll, and the papers printed. The press was about 40 feet long, and it would assemble the pages, fold them, and tie them into bundles. Quite an impressive operation. I would then load the bundles in the truck and head out for Ely, usually about 7 a.m.

I had one stop in Tower to drop off copies of the shopper portion of the newspaper and then it was on to Ely and finally to Babbitt. My part of the job ended once the papers had reached the offices, but others had to prepare them for mailing, which had to be completed before 3 p.m. to meet the Post Office schedule. Whenever we had advertising flyers, Kathie would come in to help as all of these had to be put into the newspapers by hand. I was always greeted by the sound of the address-a-graph machine pounding away, making address labels. We were very happy when the paper was finished, but then the cycle would repeat itself starting the following Monday. Somehow, on all the trips, that little truck only broke down once. I was just outside of Tower, the weather was warm, above zero, and I was able to bum a ride back to Tower to get the truck fixed. It was a miracle that I never ended up in the ditch.

Our little job of producing the Yugoslav newspaper each month turned out to be what saved me. I always marveled at how Penny could type the articles for the paper, mistake-free, even though they were in a foreign language. When I went to cash my first paycheck, it bounced due to lack of funds. Later, I would wait until we got paid for the newspaper, deposit that check and then cash my check. What a way to get paid! No matter how many ads were sold, it was obvious to me that there was no way to make the paper solvent. The pressure was mounting on the Austrengs each month, and Carol became more or more difficult to work for. Finally, in late March or early April, I simply had enough and left the paper. Shortly thereafter, Audie and Carol closed the doors on *The Ely Miner*. After more than 100 years, the paper was history. For me, it had been a good learning experience and at times fun. Somehow, we had managed to keep our heads above water for another winter.

Grief

While I was working for the Miner, the Babbitt community sent Audie and I, plus others, to Grand Rapids to attend a weeklong "Community Leadership" program conducted by the Blandon Foundation. As part of this course, we were afforded the opportunity to discuss any subject with a psychologist. Between Mike's surgery, his brief return to the resort, and the stress caused by all of this, the events had a profound effect on Kathie's and my relationship. I asked the psychologist for help. He introduced me to the concept of a "suitcase full of grief." I related that I had lost my mother in 1977, father in 1981, stepmother in 1982, and brother in

1983, and then Mike's illness in 1984, and was concerned that all of this was having a cumulative effect upon my personality and my relationship with Kathie. I was edgy and would quickly explode if things did not go exactly the way I wanted. He related that we all carry this "suitcase" and as each crisis occurs, we add it to the bag. What was critical was how we carried the suitcase. Some folks tie it around their neck and allow it to drag them down. Others try to hide the bag using a fake front. Most of us just lug it with us, making the most of it. The key point of the discussion was that this suitcase will *NEVER* go away and it's necessary to know that it was with you to allow you to cope with it. For me, this was an important step forward as it helped put things into perspective and helped me work towards improving my relationships with Mike and Kathie.

Surgery

While we were working at the Miner, Kathie came down with heavy pains in her right side. A couple of visits to our doctor in Babbitt confirmed that her appendix needed to be removed, and she underwent surgery the following day in Virginia. It turned out to be a little more complicated than anticipated as she suffered from an infection after the surgery, and it took some time for her to fully recover.

Rotary

An added benefit from the Miner job was the fact that Audie's son-in-law had been a member of the Ely Rotary Club. When he left, the club invited me to become a member. In those days, you needed to be invited to join, and I doubt I would have received such an invitation if I had not had the editor job. I continue to be a Rotarian, some 40-plus years later, and have always enjoyed my participation with Rotary. I started being involved with service organizations back at Kent State and believe that everyone needs to find a way to "give back" to their community. I also found that Rotary was a great way to network in business and have made many good business friends over the years.

We did manage to take time off to do the Indianapolis Sport Show in February. Business was getting better each year, and after leaving the Miner, our time was spent preparing for another busy summer. Mike completed his school year getting decent grades and returned to Ely to spend the summer with us. He was continuing to advance to higher plateaus but was also struggling with his speech. Therapy had helped a great deal, but he still had trouble with certain letters/sounds. I can remember "B's" being a problem. Our summer was busy and rather uneventful. My biggest concern was what we were going to do in the winter. The need to work was still a requirement.

In July, I decided to write a personal letter to the Commanding General of the US Army Finance Center. BG Virgil Richard was the Commander, and I worked for him at the Finance School back in the early 70s. I explained our circumstances and my need for work during the winter. I had no idea if the letter would even reach him. A month or so went by, and then one day, I received a phone call from the Chief of Civilian Personnel at the Center. He wasn't exactly thrilled but told me General Richards had ordered him to create a six-month temporary position for me. This was a most unusual request and created a considerable amount of work, but we discussed my availability, mid-October through mid-April, and the wheels were set in motion. Later, I was informed that I would be a GS-9, working for the Pay, Policy, and Systems Directorate. God's hand was still at work!

Our next challenge was to find a place to live during the winter. Jim let us know that good friends of ours, Bud and Ginny Beaver, who lived across the street from us in Indianapolis, may be interested in having us watch/live in their house while they were in Florida for the winter. Bud had helped Jim get his golf course job. We called, and sure enough, we were able to work out the details for our winter stay. What a relief.

The Job

The mission of Pay, Policy, and Systems was to work to make the Army's Centralized Military Pay System, JUMPS, more efficient. I was assigned as an "action officer" for a team working on the system. Thanks to my previous assignment in Centralized Pay, I understood what was expected, knew many of the key players, and was willing to act if needed. As an interesting side point, I had a full beard at the time. It was something I grew to become a "wilderness man" for the resort! Anyway, it completely changed my looks, and many people at the Center did not recognize me. I used this to my advantage by ignoring folks who I didn't care for. I was also fortunate that my bosses, both civilian employees, were easy to work with and appreciated what I could contribute to their efforts. One negative aspect of the job was that because I was a retired Regular Army Officer, I had to forfeit about 20 percent of my retired pay each month. It was a strange law designed to prevent regular officers from moving immediately into positions as a civilian federal employee. Retired reserve officers could do so without penalty. In the late 1990s, that law was dropped. Despite this loss of dollars, I was pleased to be lucky to have the six-month job. I did accumulate leave time and sick leave time which I was able to "cash" in at the end of my six months. This was also a big help.

Other Items

The remainder of the winter was pretty much routine. Kathie worked part-time at a dress shop. Jim continued his work and schooling, while Mike had a good year at Ball State. We also started a Christmas routine of going to Cleveland to be with Kathie's mom. The boys would also come. It was a fun time for everyone.

Jim's girlfriend, Lisa, had gone on to Indiana University, and they started to grow apart. Jim was living with a guy in a two-bedroom apartment and fell for his roommate's girlfriend, Kim. When the roommate found out what was happening, he locked Jim out of the apartment. Jim had to break down the door to retrieve his personal items, and he and Kim moved into another apartment nearby. Both Kathie and I felt that Kim would someday become our daughter-in-law, as Jim told us it was a case of "bells and whistles" when they met. Jim was completing his two-year degree in Law Enforcement and began talking about applying to become a police officer. A friend recommended that he continue his education, and he decided to enroll at Indiana/Purdue University (IUPUI) in Indianapolis to complete a four-year degree in Criminal Justice. Kim also started at IUPUI working towards a degree in Communications.

We all worked our booth at the Indianapolis Sport Show in February 1987. The show was good, and we enjoyed watching Mike talk with potential customers. While he was still recovering from his ordeal and still taking speech therapy at school, he was able to carry on good conversations with the folks stopping at our booth to ask questions. It was another positive sign that he reached yet another plateau in his long road to recovery. Our booth location was now on the main floor of the Coliseum, and business was brisk. Our repeat business had also increased so we were confident that the summer of 1987 business would be good.

As my six months ended, I was pleased to receive a special cash award for the work I had done (always good to get cash!) and assurances that if funding for the position was available in October, I would be hired again. What a relief even with the caveat about funding for the next fiscal year. Mike decided to accept a job in New York as a camp counselor for handicapped kids for a couple of months. He would be a senior when he returned to Ball State in the fall. Jim was in ROTC and would spend six weeks of his summer at Ft. Lewis, WA.

As we got ready to leave, Jim said he could get us a deal on a used golf cart at the golf course he was working at. We somehow managed to load the cart inside our van and headed off to Ely. The cart proved to be a great addition to the resort.

The Resort

Thanks to our good fortune with the winter jobs, we decided to make some major improvements to the resort. I decided to add screen porches to the front of each cabin. I hired Bob Koschak, who built our docks, to do the work, and he worked hard and did a wonderful job. We were able to get them built before the real start of the season, Memorial Day. Kathie and I painted them and touched up paint on the cabins. When we went to turn on the water, we were rewarded with minimal leaks as we'd done a much better job the previous fall getting the water lines drained. It was a very busy six weeks and a happy one. Really our first summer when only the two of us were operating the resort.

The Weekly Routine

Our weeks ran from Saturday afternoon to Saturday morning. On Friday, I would cut all of the grass, and then on Saturday morning, as our guests departed, we began working on cleaning cabins, setting up boats, etc., making everything ready for the new guests who would start arriving that afternoon. Saturday was a wild day.

Through trial and error, we learned to place everything we needed in a large garbage bag the night before. The bags would be labeled with the cabin number. We would fill the bag with clean sheets, TP, clean bathroom rugs, kitchen bags, etc. We had a box set up with cleaning materials and thanks to the golf cart, we would load everything for the cabin to be cleaned and head off. Our tasks were also divided. Kathie cleaned the bathrooms and kitchen. I would strip the beds, make them, vacuum, and clean the Weber grills. Fortunately, most of our guests left the cabins in reasonable shape and we were able to clean most cabins in less than an hour. Kathie baked batches of chocolate chip cookies on Friday, and we would have a dozen fresh cookies waiting when our guests arrived. They were an immediate hit!

We then repeated the cycle until all the cabins were completed. Usually, we were able to start before 7 a.m, and if all went well, we finished around noon. The dump closed at noon on Saturday, so I also had to work in a dump run during the morning. Assuming we were in good shape, I would then spend time cleaning our boats, setting them up with outboard motors and gasoline, and placing them on the proper dock.

When folks made reservations, they would request a

motor, so I knew what size motor, etc. A boat was included in the rental fee so if they brought their own boat, I towed ours back to the boathouse. Sometimes cleaning the boats was a mess as there would be fish blood, dried worms, etc., all over them. Guests would keep the cabins clean but not the boats! Again, thanks to the golf cart, heavy duties such as lugging 6-gallon gas tanks were made much easier. If we were lucky, we would have everything ready, be able to shower, and eat a quick sandwich before the new customers would start arriving. For those years when we only had the five cabins, we were somehow able to do the chores without having to hire additional help. By Saturday night, we were both dragging! It also became a Saturday night tradition to have a homemade pizza after all our guests arrived and were settled into their cabins. Some weeks we had pizza by 7 p.m., while a few times it was after 10 p.m. before the "nest was full."

The rest of the week also had an informal routine. Sunday was spent getting everyone settled, making sure everything was good in the cabins, boats, motors, etc. We held our fishing seminar on Sunday evening. On Monday, preparation for the following week would begin. Kathie would take all the laundry into Ely and use the Laundromat to wash it. We had learned early on that the septic system for the house would not handle the water from a washer. This would take all morning because at times at least a half dozen washers were needed to complete the job. She would then lug everything home and start drying things in our dryer.

Tuesday evening, we had our cookout. We did this at the screen house and turned our ping pong table into a serving table. The weather at times made the cookouts exciting, but for the most part we managed to get them in. If it was really raining, we'd postpone things until Wednesday evening. Wednesday was also dump day so I would go to each cabin and pick up garbage. I also cleaned our fish in the cleaning house each morning and it was great getting everything to the dump. By keeping everything picked up, we cut down on our visits from bears. Of course, everyone wanted to see a black bear, but they really created a mess if they got into a full garbage can. Fortunately, over all the years we were there we never had a raccoon problem. Guests were pretty much on their own for much of the week. There were attractions in Ely plus a good assortment of restaurants when mom needed a break from cooking. Then the cycle repeated itself on Saturday.

On occasion, I'd sneak off and do a little fishing. My story to Kathie was I needed to know what was going on so I could talk intelligently about fishing with the guests. It worked! Early in the year when we were not busy, Kathie would join me. I got her into casting artificial lures for smallmouth bass. In the spring, the big fish would come into the shallow water to spawn, and we could be very successful. The bass would hit a top water lure and jump immediately. I loved to hear Kathie yell when she got a strike. She was a good fisherman. We both loved those brief times together on the lake. In addition to maybe catching a fish or two, we both loved the water, the loons, and the sheer beauty of our lake. Bob loved to join us, and his ears would fly as the boat moved through the water. Great memories.

While Jim was in ROTC Summer Camp, Kim visited her relatives in California to see if she wanted to go to school out there. She ended up meeting Jim at Fort Lewis at the end of his camp, and they returned to Indianapolis together. We knew then, for sure, that wedding bells were in their future. Jim and I also exchanged letters that summer. He wrote expressing all his frustrations concerning how things had gone in his life. He was disappointed about not being able to attend Indiana University, and many of my decisions seemed to go against him. I responded as best I could, trying to explain why I did what I did. This seemed to help clear the air, and while I'm sure he was not happy with my decisions, at least he knew why I had made them. Mike's time as a counselor had gone well, and he was able to spend a short time with us before returning to Ball State.

Our year had been good, and we were happy to put the resort "to sleep" after another successful summer. I checked with the Finance Center and found out that my job had again been created, and I would be able to return to work in the same Directorate. I also learned that I would be a GS-11 versus the GS-9 from last year, which meant a significant pay increase. The Beavers again agreed to allow us to house-sit for the winter. The only change there was we would also have to care for their two cocker spaniels. It was a happy time when we headed out for Indianapolis that fall.

Indianapolis

Things went well that winter. The job was good as I already knew what was happening and fit in without difficulty. The best part was doing basically the same thing but at a higher rate of pay. Kathie continued to work at the dress shop, so we were busy and happy.

We had decided to make a new sign for the resort, so by using a vu-graph at work, I was able to make a large pattern for the sign. Our brochure had a large circle with a scene of a cabin, dock, pine trees, and streaks in the sky. The streaks represented the Northern Lights. This is what I used as a pattern. Fort Harrison had a craft shop with all kinds of woodworking equipment, and I cut out the pattern in plywood. We then mounted it on a 4' x 8' sheet of plywood. The final step was painting in the design and mounting the letters for our name. Everything went quite well together, and we used that sign for the remainder of our time at the resort.

We again spent the Christmas holiday with Kathie's mom, Hilda, in Cleveland. Hilda just loved Christmas and was a joy to watch as we passed out gifts. She and Ralf were great buddies, and she was really enjoying life, and we all enjoyed those times with her. Mike had come with us, and Jim brought Kim in his latest car. It was a big Ford Mustang which he loved. On the way back to Indianapolis, the roads were snowy, and ice-covered in some places. At the end of one stretch, there was a stop sign and to our horror, Jim and Kim slid through the intersection in front of us on a patch of ice. Fortunately, no one was at the intersection, and Jim regained control. Hearts in our mouths for a few brief moments.

After another successful Sport Show, plus good bookings throughout the winter, we knew the next summer would be busy.

Graduation

The "main" event of our stay in Indianapolis that year was Mike's graduation from Ball State in May 1987. His senior year had been very productive. He had been elected President of his dormitory for the year, a solid recognition that the "new" Mike had arrived. His degree was in General Studies, but he expressed hope that someday he would be able to work with, and maybe even teach, "special" children. I had already finished my job and returned to the resort, but we drove down for the big event with Audie, Carol, and their grandson Chris.

Graduation had been a major event for Mike. While he was hospitalized in Florida, we used Mitch's graduation date, in May, as a goal for him to be well enough to leave the hospital. I made a sign with the date of her graduation on it and hung it so that Mike could see it from his bed. When times were tough, we would all concentrate on that date and use it as inspiration for Mike to work hard. Sure enough, Mike attended Mitch's graduation in May 1984.

Now it was his turn to graduate, and it was a very proud day for everyone. Mike had taken another camp counselor job for the first two months of the summer. When we returned to the resort, he left for the camp. He was driving on his own and after the job was completed, he visited with longtime friends in Washington, DC, and Massachusetts.

25th Anniversary

We started our celebration by renewing our wedding vows. It was a happy time, and the pastor was challenged as he had never been involved with a vow renewal. Members of Kathie's sewing club threw a small party, complete with a pool (kids' wading pool) and cardboard palm trees that they set up in front of the house. Quite an event.

Since everything had happened, Kathie and I had not even thought about a vacation. However, we decided to celebrate our 25th anniversary in style. We had spent a lot of time in Florida but never in the Keys. After some research, we rented a room for a few days at Hawk's Cay Resort on Duck Key. Never forget those names! It turned out to be quite an adventure. To save time, we flew into Tampa and rented a car from Alamo.

I should have known we were in trouble when we walked through the rental parking lot, and I saw this old car parked in the corner with grass growing underneath it. Sure enough, that was the car that was brought to us, a Chevy compact of some sort. We were on the Interstate in Tampa about 15 minutes out from the rental agency, and I noticed the "overheat" light on. Sure enough, in a few hundred yards, there was smoke trailing behind the car. I had no choice but to continue as we were on an overpass with no shoulders. By the time I got to where I could pull off, the car made a horrible sound and quit running. I think I "cooked" the engine.

One hour into our trip and stranded on the Interstate

in the days before cell phones. We happened to be in one of Tampa's roughest neighborhoods, but I saw a business nearby. It was surrounded by barb wire but there were cars parked by it. I left Kathie with the car, and after climbing the wire fence along the Interstate, I finally got someone to open the door so that I could call Alamo. When I got back to the car, Kathie told me three people had stopped to help, a nice surprise.

Finally, a tow truck appeared with a car, and we were able to start our vacation. The car ran well, and we did make it to Duck Key. When we went to check-in, our room wasn't ready, so we were given complementary drinks at the bar. A couple of drinks later, we were told the room was ready. I sent Kathie up to the room while I went to get our suitcases. Would you believe it, when I got to the car there were the keys in the ignition and of course the car was locked. I was bummed and upset at the same time. Returning to the office, I contacted a locksmith, but it was past 5 p.m. so that meant another $50 to make the service call. The hotel had an intercom system, and while I was waiting for the locksmith, a call came over the system saying a guest had broken a key off in a room lock. The room number was ours. Wow! I had visions of Kathie being so upset about us having to wait that she had broken the key. Turns out this was not the case as the broken key was in the lock when she arrived at the room. When we finally settled into the room, it was a relief, and we had a good laugh.

We enjoyed the area quite a bit, especially the water and real Key Lime pie! I must confess that I felt Key West was very overrated and later in life when our cruise ship made a stop there, we did leave the ship. At least we had a 25th Anniversary we'd long remember.

The Resort

Our summer was extremely busy. After our first few years struggling to find business, we found ourselves full for the months of June, July, and August. These weeks were needed each year to make the payments on the resort and the extra land. Thanks to our winter work, we were able to cover the land payment and then plow the dollars received during the summer into resort improvements and the resort payment. Our resort payment was due at the end of the season, and we took great pride in handing the $15,000 check to the realtor as a sign that we were a success.

The Wedding

Jim announced that he and Kim were engaged and wanted to be married at the resort over the Labor Day weekend. We agreed and did not accept reservations for that week. After all the rough times Jim had experienced over the last few years, I wanted to do everything I could to make his marriage ceremony everything that he wanted. We sent the word out as well as invitations and soon found out it would be a gala event. Kathie's mom and aunt would attend as would Jerry and JoAnn and all my relatives from the DC area. Much fun planning would be required.

The site of the wedding would be a small flat area down by the dock for Cabins 3 and 4 right on the lake. One big problem with the site was that a rock-filled path led from Cabin 4 down to the lake. Not an appropriate aisle for the bride to walk down. I contacted Bob Koschak, the man who'd built our screen porches and asked him to build wooden steps down to the lake. He did a wonderful job and he also built steps down from Cabin 1 down to our beach/dock area. A major improvement to the resort as well as a great aisle for our bride.

The summer flew by and as the day approached, it seemed like we spent more time preparing for the wedding than taking care of our guests! Not really. Jeff and Lori Shulze, owners of our neighboring resort, Timber Wolf Lodge (formerly called The Escape) agreed to let us use their now-closed restaurant for the rehearsal dinner. Over the years we became close friends with Lori and Jeff. Kathie, with Lori helping, prepared the food for the dinner. We made reservations at another resort in the area for the wedding dinner/reception. I also arranged for the rental of a houseboat for three days for their honeymoon at yet another resort. The pastor at the church Mike, Audie, and Carol attended agreed to perform the ceremony and we even were able to borrow the church organ and sound system for the wedding.

There was a small hillside leading to the site and we bought several hay bales to place along the side of the hill to be our seats. A platform also needed to be built over a small depression to allow the entire wedding party to have room for the ceremony. It was a fun time, and everyone was excited and happy as they began to arrive and fill up the resort. By the time everyone had arrived the resort was full. Kim's father, brother, and sisters came in as did my two sisters-in-law, niece and nephew plus Kathie's cousin, mom, and aunt. Other family friends arrived from Cleveland and Jerry and JoAnn also appeared with their trailer. Jim had selected Mike as his best man and had even located an old buddy from Fort Lewis and got him to come and join the wedding party.

The rehearsal dinner was great fun, and both families presented a slide show of the bride and groom in their younger years. Great food, thanks to Kathie's efforts, lots to drink and plenty of fun. I hired a friend to video the event which also kept everyone on their toes. The rehearsal itself went well ending with the wedding party throwing the bride and groom into the lake.

We awoke the next morning to rain beating down. What to do? Our alternate location was the pastor's church in Babbitt, but we'd agreed to hang tough until that afternoon and see what the weather would do. A couple of hours before the wedding, the skies cleared, and the wedding went off without a problem. We were also concerned about strangers bringing their boats down the lake to see what was happening but none of this happened. The lake was quiet and as smooth as glass throughout. The reception was at Silver Rapids Lodge about twenty miles from our place. After the reception was finished, our plan was to have a float plane fly Jim and Kim to their houseboat on Birch Lake. However, about halfway through the reception, the skies opened up and rain poured down. The pilot called and canceled the trip. The alternate plan was for the kids to drive down to the resort that had the houseboat and have the owner take them to the boat which had already been anchored in a secluded bay on Birch Lake.

While all of this was happening, the pastor was organizing a "shivaree." This was a term used in Minnesota for a group to go harass the bride and groom at their honeymoon site. There were three boats available, and we all agreed to meet at the Birch Lake landing about an hour after the kids had left the reception. The "attack" was meant to happen as the storm stopped when we reached the landing. After a 30-minute boat ride, the three boats silently moved around the houseboat. We had brought bottle rockets, pots and pans, and other noise makers. All at once, the solitude of the quiet bay erupted with a "bang." It took a while, but finally Jim and Kim appeared on deck and after wishing them well, the "raiding" party disappeared into the night. After we got the boats back on the trailers, the storm returned with a vengeance. What a great way to end a great wedding.

Before I leave the wedding, I must tell of the story of Hilda and Nanny, Kathie's mom and aunt. They were both in their 80s, not over 5 feet tall with wonderful white hair. We set them and Nanny's daughter, Betty, up in Cabin 2. Kathie got such a kick out of walking down to their cabin each evening and "tucking" them in for the night. Those two little white heads peeking out from underneath the covers. Memories to be cherished. For them, being in the woods and being part of the wedding was a great experience.

As everyone left following the wedding, we settled into getting ready for another winter in Indianapolis. Mike had accepted a position as a teacher's helper for a Special Education school which was located on the same campus as his high school. He and another friend from high school would share the rent on a small house. Jim was starting to close in on his degree and continued school in the evening as well as working.

In early October, I got word that the job would be

available, so our next task was finding a place to live. The Beavers, due to health concerns, were not returning to Florida so we had to look elsewhere.

Over the past couple of years, Kathie and I had become good friends with Indianapolis guests, Bill and Bertha Thompson, and I always enjoyed fishing with Bill. One year we got to make a day trip to Basswood Lake and had a good, lucky day catching some nice walleyes. Bill was thrilled. I always worried about his health as he was a heavy smoker and at times struggled with his breathing. In addition to their time at the resort, we would also see them on occasion during our winters. Bill and Bertha worked at the Finance Center, so I was able to visit with them while we were working. Bill's son worked for Shell Oil and owned a home on the west side of Indianapolis. One day when we were discussing future living arrangements for the coming winter, Bill said the son's home would be vacant and that his son would be happy to let us live in the home during our stay. For once, our housing situation was settled early.

Indianapolis

We made the move to Indianapolis. The new house was located on the west side of town, and we had to learn how to travel back and forth to work. Kathie found a job at a local Kroger store. My work was a continuation of the tasks I had worked on, and I was able to settle into my routine quickly.

The previous summer, we had started the practice of leaving critique sheets in the cabins. Among other questions, we asked them to provide a favorite recipe, maybe the one they had used for our cookouts. We put these recipes together and *"Northern Lights Delights"* was born. We learned that the Minnesota term for casserole was hot dish and many recipes used Cool Whip. We included our first issue with our annual Christmas cards to our previous year's guests. It was a fun project and over the years we reached a point where we published our own cookbook. Unfortunately, printing costs ended the project. Our guests really enjoyed being part of the project and loved seeing their names and hometowns in print.

In January, I noticed an ad in the paper for people to work for H & R Block during the upcoming tax season. I investigated the ad and found out that about six weeks of classwork was required before beginning work. Classes were held in the evenings, twice a week and I decided to enroll and see if I'd like the work. I found that my old accounting background helped, and I enjoyed the classes and learned a great deal about taxes. When we graduated, we had the option of working with customers at a retail store preparing the returns or working in Block's centralized processing center. The center was located near the Finance Center, and I opted to work there. Today returns are computerized and filed electronically but then everything was paper. My job was to review returns made by the preparers and ensure everything was proper before they were submitted to IRS. I worked two or three evenings a week after my regular job.

One evening we invited Jim and Kim for dinner, and they asked if they could bring someone else with them. We, of course, said "yes" and they appeared with a wonderful little puppy - Wosha - a chocolate Lab. Jim got the name from the Amharic word for "dog" that he learned while we were living in Ethiopia. We had a "grand puppy!"

The Resort

Upon our return to the resort, we started work on making more improvements. During the winter, we spent a lot of time discussing what improvements to make at the resort. The screen porches on the cabins had been popular but many times were used by guests to store extra gear rather than for enjoyment. After looking things over, we decided to "open" up the cabins by removing the wall facing the porch. To do this, we would have to replace the screens with glass. We also carpeted the porch floors. Thanks again to the help of Bob Koschak, we were able to get this done before

Memorial Day. The change to the cabins was remarkable. We had in effect added another room to each cabin and our guests loved the change.

We also started the process of updating the bathrooms in Cabins 1, 2, 3, and 4. They had been added to each cabin and the interior walls were half-log, always collecting dust and dirt. They had old-style metal showers with a concrete base and old fixtures. Once we had a guest accidentally unscrew the lever for the hot water and came screaming up to the office that the bathroom was being flooded. The plumbing for the showers and commodes was also exposed. Bill Wright, the husband of Kathie's cousin Betty, was a very good handyman and one summer he and I redid the bathroom in Cabin 1. We removed the fixtures and paneled the walls with white, plastic sheets, replaced the shower, and the sink with an up-to-date vanity, medicine cabinet and rerouted the plumbing under the cabin. Using the knowledge gained from Bill, I was then able to do similar updates to our remaining cabins.

Army Worms

Mike remained in Indianapolis and worked various part-time jobs. He did visit us to help me celebrate my 50th birthday. While an important milestone, 1989 was also the summer of the Army worms. The worms – Forest Tent Caterpillars – were with us each year but periodically when the conditions were right, the population exploded. Such was the case that year. I had never heard of them and first discovered the outbreak driving to Ely. The car ahead of me suddenly started weaving back and forth, and then I saw the huge areas in the road covered with worms. Guess he was trying to run them over. They were everywhere and gathered in large balls of worms as they ate every leaf on a tree. It was a remarkable sight driving into the resort with the balls of worms hanging from the trees. Stephen King could have written a book!

We celebrated my birthday during our weekly cookout at the screen house. As everyone sat in the grass eating, there was at least one worm on every blade. Kathie's sewing club ladies appeared to sing Happy Birthday and got quite a kick watching me put on the size 50 bra they had brought for the occasion!

The worms were also a challenge for our guests. Most of the women walked outside with rain caps on their heads in case a worm dropped into their hair. We found that Yard Guard would kill them and each Saturday morning we would spray the front of each cabin so they would not be there to greet our arriving guests. The reactions to the worms varied from utter disgust to one mother telling us that her little ones had only eaten three that morning; she called them protein!

As time passed, large brown flies emerged from the

caterpillars. They loved to swarm on the warm aluminum of our boats. Again, quite a sight but at least the flies did not bite. Before it was over, almost every tree with leaves had been stripped bare. Fortunately, the trees quickly recovered once the invasion was finished.

As a funny side note, our neighbor resort, Timber Wolf Lodge, would periodically host groups attending activities at the new Wolf Center in Ely. One evening after our weekly cookout, we heard a lot of "wolf howling" coming from down the lake. Turned out that the wolf group next door was "howling" to see if they could get a real wolf to answer. Some of our guests started howling, and the folks next door thought they were being answered, a great laugh for everyone!

Jim and Kim also spent time with us at the resort. They were really into water sports, and I was able to borrow Audie's boat while they were with us so that they could water ski. I also put the boys to work helping me shovel gravel from a nearby pit into our truck and then spreading loads along our road. Between rain, traffic, etc., maintenance of the road was a continual battle.

My job held up for another winter and things were under control as we closed the resort after another successful summer. Annual payments had been made and we were about out from under the medical bills accumulated with Mike. Financially things were starting to return to normal, and we made plans to buy new outboard motors for our rental fleet. Again, we had to find a new place to live for the winter as Bill's son had returned to Indianapolis and his house was not available.

Indianapolis

As time was running out, our good friends, Rep and Mary Repischak, offered us the use of their spare bedroom for the winter. We agonized over whether to accept, but finally agreed to give it a try. It was going to be quite a challenge to live together for that long of a time and remain friends.

Fortunately, we were all working. Kathie took a job with a local supermarket. Rep was working for a private firm, and Mary and I worked at the Finance Center. Kathie and I both worked on Saturday, which gave Rep and Mary some space together. Somehow, Kathie and Mary were able to coexist in the kitchen. They worked out a deal where one would be responsible for the meal one evening, then the other would do it the next day. Leftovers were also worked in as full meals. Bob was with us and really helped. He only demanded a walk in the morning and one in the evening and then would provide comic relief during the evenings. The most difficult part was that Kathie and I only had one bedroom to ourselves. At times, things got rather tense just from the day-to-day activities.

Mike also contributed to this unease. While he seemed to enjoy his work, I think he felt frustrated being without many friends and living in less than great surroundings. We tried to have him for dinner whenever possible, but there were times when he would take his frustration out on us. One time he blamed us for his aneurysm, saying that since it was congenital, it was our fault that he was born with it. At another time, he announced that we owed him $10,000 to repay him for the money he saved us because he had the college scholarship. Such comments hurt me to the core, and I would react negatively. Kathie would then rush to Mike's defense, and we'd become frustrated with each other. Without our privacy at home, we were unable to argue things out, and there were times when the frustration remained "bottled up" for a long period. One time when things were particularly tense, I rented a room in a nearby hotel so that we could just vent to each other in private. It really helped us to release the tension and realize where each one of us stood on various conflicts.

The winter at work went well. I spent most of my time working on the development of new codes which when added to the pay system would allow Finance Offices to track the location of soldiers. The Army was using

"Task Forces" for specific missions. These would be put together by combining units from various organizations. Many times, small units would be assigned away from their parent organization, and the Finance support unit would lose track of the unit's location. This could and did cause many problems. The result was that the new codes eliminated the problems, and I could at least tell myself I had been able to contribute a little to the mission.

I decided to work again for H & R Block and started classes after the Christmas/New Year holidays. My time with H & R Block was much more rewarding this year. Last year I'd learned the system within the central processing office and this year I made sure that I was assigned to the area that prepared out-of-state tax returns. Rather than being paid by the hour, I was paid by the number of returns I prepared. A different rate was paid for different states. I soon learned that states like California could become quite complicated with each return requiring significant research. On the other hand, states like Illinois, very common in Indiana, were very easy. When I arrived each evening, I would search through the pile of returns pulling all the Illinois returns plus other states that were also relatively easy. Then it was a matter of really concentrating and pumping out the returns. Suddenly I found myself making between $15 and $20 per hour versus the $5 I'd made the previous year. My two months of work really helped add to our bottom line.

Jim and Kim bought a new house, and Jim graduated from the police academy and started his career with the department. Mike continued to work as a teacher's assistant through the winter. He was better but still not happy with the course his life had taken. We again spent a wonderful Christmas with Hilda in Cleveland. She was full of it and really enjoyed having us with her, and we really enjoyed being with her.

Hilda

In late March 1990, Kathie got a call from her cousin Betty in Cleveland that Hilda had fallen while walking Ralf. She immediately left for Cleveland, and when she arrived, Hilda was not doing well. Later that evening, Kathie called 911, and at the hospital, they determined that Hilda had suffered a stroke. That weekend, I joined Kathie in Cleveland, and we were happy that Hilda was responding to treatment and seemed to be on the road to recovery. We talked about having her join us at the resort for the summer, and then if needed, we'd spend the next winter with her in Cleveland. I returned to work while Kathie remained in Cleveland. Unfortunately, a couple of days later, Hilda suffered another very deep stroke and slipped into a coma. It soon became apparent that she was not going to recover, and Kathie was then forced to search for a nursing home. After a couple of weeks during which Hilda made no progress, Kathie reluctantly returned to Indy as we were preparing to return to the resort. This was our first significant exposure to problems associated with the expense of nursing homes. Social Security covered 100 days of care, but after that, the burden fell upon the surviving family. Because Hilda was the lone survivor of her family, i.e., no living husband, the government, by law, could seize her home and other assets to pay for her long-term care. We were fortunate that Hilda had given ownership of her home to Kathie earlier. There was no way to predict how long Hilda would live, so there was no choice but to wait.

An unfortunate side effect of this disappointment was Ralf. When Hilda was first taken to the hospital, Ralf went "crazy." He tore up items in the house, even attacking the metal Venetian blinds in the living room. He could not stay alone at home, and Kathie was worried about giving him up for adoption due to his destructive behavior. After consulting with the veterinarian, she made the decision to have him put down. What a sad day for her.

We enjoyed another productive Sport Show, and again reservations held strong for the coming season. When my job ended, we prepared to return to Ely. As usual, our van was loaded to the roof with supplies for the resort. I am sure drivers passing us got many laughs passing the van loaded with rolls of toilet paper and a happy dog, Bob. As we departed, we felt happy that we were very lucky to still be great friends with Rep and Mary. We remain so to this day.

The Resort

We returned to the resort with a heavy heart. Kathie's cousin Betty and her aunt, Nanny, visited Hilda weekly and reported no change. It was a difficult time for Kathie as she felt guilty for not being at her mom's side yet understood there was nothing to be done. Hilda remained in a deep coma, unaware of her surroundings. We considered ourselves lucky in that prior to all this happening, Hilda had passed ownership of the house to Kathie and added her name to various small bank accounts. Dad had done the same for me prior to his death, and those actions certainly helped when the time came to resolve her estate.

Water

The summer had been particularly hot and dry, and the lake level had fallen a good two feet by the middle of July. Our main well was a shallow, lake water well. It provided good water, tested annually by the Department of Health. One day, the water just stopped.

Wow, what to do? Fortunately, the commodes were on the lake water system and continued to function. I raced down to the well, lifted the cover to the pit and the cover to the well. No Water! Kathie rushed to town and bought jugs of bottled water for each cabin, and folks thought it was a "fun" idea to take their baths in the lake until we resolved the problem. Fortunately, in an earlier summer, I had discovered an old sand point well about fifty yards from the main well. For whatever reason, probably anticipating such a problem, we hooked up an old pump to the well and ran power to it. My only chance was that the well would produce enough water to get us by. A sand point well is simply a pipe with a copper point on the end that is driven into the ground. The point has holes in it. I had never run it, but it did produce a small amount of dirty brown water when I started the pump. It was obvious that the flow was insufficient.

Then, I got the idea to fire my .22 caliber pistol down the pipe. I'd remember reading or hearing that the concussion of the round could break up the sand and improve the flow of water. Would you believe it worked! Water gushed from the pipe and soon turned clear as all the sand was removed. We were back in business about six hours after the problem had started. What good luck and I was proud of myself for taking the time earlier to have the second well ready for such an emergency. Later in the fall, the rains came, the lake level rose, and water gushed back into our main well. A good lesson learned.

We encountered many more problems including storm damage, dock problems, leaking boats, damaged motors, dripping faucets, temperamental gas pilot lights in water heaters and stoves, and many more over the years. As owners, our guests expected us to be able to resolve their problems immediately and this was always a major challenge. Somehow, over the years, we learned from our mistakes and became able to resolve most issues without having to call in outside help.

Graduation/Commissioning

In May 1990, Jim was going to graduate from IUPUI and receive his commission as a 2 Lt. in the Army through ROTC. Jim asked me to commission him during the ceremony. I was very pleased that he wanted me to do this, and we dug out my Dress Blue uniform for the occasion. I also had to shave, the first time since I retired in 1983. It was a quick trip back to Indy, but a great ceremony, and I was very proud to pin on Jim's gold bars. He thought briefly about applying for active duty but opted to become part of the Indiana National Guard after he completed the Military Police Basic course that summer. Once he returned from that school, he applied for and was accepted into the Indianapolis Police Department. As a side note, my full beard really changed my appearance. When I returned to Ely and went to my first Rotary Club meeting without the beard, I was asked if I needed a "visitor" card as no one recognized me. I started regrowing my beard!

Hilda

On the 19th of August 1990, we got the call from Betty that Hilda had passed away. It was the 99th day of her confinement to the nursing home. We were able to have friends watch the resort and flew to Cleveland for her funeral. The boys drove up from Indy to be with us. It was a happy/sad day. Happy that Hilda was finally at peace. Happy that we all had wonderful memories of her, especially in her later years. Sad to have lost her. We all discussed what to do with the house and finally decided that Kathie and I would spend the winter in Cleveland getting the place ready for sale. My time working winters at the Finance Center was over.

Cleveland

Once we got the year tied up at the resort, we made it to Cleveland in November. Al and Hilda had built the house in the 40s, and while Al had done a lot of work over the years on the house, it still needed several improvements. It was a sad time for Kathie going through all of Hilda's things but also a time of discovery as we found lots of interesting things that Al had put away over the years. The basement had been Al's domain, and it was packed with every kind of nail, screw, pieces of leftover wood, tools, and other small treasures. It even had a small bedroom and bath which needed a lot of work. We soon decided that the entire basement needed to be painted. A real challenge with all the stuff crammed into it. The garage was in a similar shape so lots of time was spent weeding things out. Each week the garbage men picked up lots of unwanted treasures.

The house also needed a lot of work. We knew it had hardwood floors so decided to just remove the old carpet. The floors turned out to be in great shape and added a lot to the warm, cozy feeling of the place. The dishwasher hadn't worked in years and Bill Wright, Betty's husband, helped install a new one. The bathroom tile also needed lots of work, so we decided to replace the tile with a tub insert. There were numerous cracks in the ceilings and walls which needed patching and painting. Our winter was a busy one as funds were short and we did almost everything ourselves.

The holiday season turned out to be rather traumatic. Both of us had assumed that we would be included in Betty and Nanny's holiday celebration for Christmas.

The boys were going to join us after Christmas. Jim needed to spend the day with Kim's side of the family. Mike got involved with a homeless project and spent the first part of the season helping feed them for Christmas. Betty's family always celebrated Christmas on Christmas Eve. A couple of days prior, Kathie assuming we were included, asked what she could bring for dinner. Betty rather abruptly informed her that their celebration was "family only." What a stunning revelation. Kathie was Betty's only living relative in the United States but not considered to be part of the family. She was crushed and I was unhappy. We ended up going to see the movie *"Dances with Wolves,"* attending Christmas Eve services at church, and enjoying a nice dinner at home. We still "get along" with Betty but this incident will, unfortunately, never be forgotten.

When the boys arrived, we had a fun time and spent a lot of time talking about Hilda's home and deciding what, if anything, the boys wanted from the house. They both spent a lot of time there and I found it interesting to see what items were of interest to each one. Mike wanted many of Al's tools which made sense because he and Al had spent some good times working on projects in the basement. He also wanted a bookcase that was built-in to the wall in Al's attic bedroom. Mike still has the bookcase in his home. They both returned to Indianapolis with several small items.

We again had our booth at the Indianapolis Sport Show. It gave us time to visit with the boys and business, as usual, was good for the resort. While we were there, Mike introduced us to his new girlfriend, Amanda. He indicated that he was serious about marrying her in the spring. This came as quite a surprise and we had long and hard talks with Mike about his plans. Amanda was some ten years older than he and we were concerned that neither had a solid career nor solid plans for the future. Amanda quickly proved to be a person who was difficult to like. We had wanted to celebrate her birthday at our favorite Chinese place, but she rejected it as not being nice enough and selected another place significantly more expensive with poorer food than our place. We talked with them in detail and told them upfront that we didn't think it was a good match for either one of them. We returned to Cleveland not knowing which way Mike would go.

Another big challenge was getting the estate resolved legally. We hired the family lawyer, which turned out to be a mistake as he proved to be rather incompetent and only wanted to send us bills for his service. Despite the problems, matters were resolved and when spring arrived, we were ready to put the house on the market. We wanted the house to move quickly so set a reasonable price. Looking back, it must have been too reasonable as the house sold the first week it was on the market. We had decided to split all proceeds from Hilda's estate three ways, which was in accordance with her desires. Each share was a little over $20,000.

With the house sold, it was time to return to our home, Northern Lights Lodge. We now knew that this would be our long-term home as winter jobs would no longer be available. We rented a small U-Haul truck and cleaned everything out of the house. On our way home, we stopped in Indianapolis to drop off items for Jim and Mike before heading north.

The Resort

In addition to working on Hilda's house, we spent lots of time discussing our future plans for the resort. One idea was to build on to the front of the house. The house only had about 800 square feet of living space, with the basement being mostly dedicated to business. I designed a large single-floor addition to run the full length of the house, some 35 feet. It would be 12 feet wide and have a large stone fireplace. That would be our remembrance of Hilda. I contracted with a local builder, Darwin Lossing, to do the construction. The father of the owners of our neighbor resort, Timber Wolf Lodge, did concrete work and fireplaces. He laid the pad for the addition and built the fireplace.

During the initial construction phase, Bob provided the entertainment. We had a large flower bed in front of the house. We found through trial and error that impatiens loved to grow there. There were many chipmunks in the area which Bob loved to hunt. However, we had trained him not to enter the flower bed and it became a sanctuary for the chipmunks. If they made it to the flower bed, they were safe. Well, the flower bed had to go when it was time to pour the pad and as the workers dug, the chipmunks exploded, and Bob was in "dog heaven." That one day he dispatched over a dozen, stopping work many times as everyone watched the carnage. Chipmunks are very prolific so even with all his work we still maintained a good population of critters. You could almost see Bob "smiling" that day as he took his vengeance on the ones who had been saved by the flower bed!

About this time, Jerry and JoAnn arrived for a brief visit and they were able to watch the addition start to take shape. One morning it rained buckets, and we awoke to find water running in the front door. The 2 x 4 foot footings around the pad were acting as a dam holding all the rainwater. Jerry and I managed to cut out a section of the footings so the water could drain without flooding the downstairs of the house.

One morning during their visit, I was returning from a walk down our road and as I neared the house, I heard all this yelling. Somehow, a squirrel had gotten into the house and as I reached the second floor, there was Jerry and JoAnn standing on chairs, yelling at Bob to catch the squirrel. What a sight, Jerry was about 6'4", a 30-year Army veteran with combat experience on that chair. A good laugh. We finally cornered the squirrel in the bathroom and ended the encounter thanks to Bob as he knew where the guy was despite the many hiding places in the house.

We enjoyed Jerry and JoAnn so much and hated to see them leave.

To save money, Kathie and I decided to panel the interior of the addition ourselves. Al had a large radial arm saw which we had brought to the resort, and it allowed us to easily cut the pieces of tongue and groove knotty pine paneling. We added electric baseboard heaters but planned on heating the entire downstairs with the large new fireplace. It was quite a project as there were many odd sized corners which needed special cuts and at times it was like completing a jigsaw puzzle. It was early in the spring, and we had great fun working together on the project and watching everything come together. We also removed the front of the office, the front door, and a window next to the front door. The finished project really added a total "woodsy" effect to our home. We loved it.

I also asked Bob Koschak to build a deck around the

entire addition. It was eight feet wide and turned out to be a wonderful addition. We also had large flower boxes built for the railings that surrounded the deck. Kathie soon learned that begonias loved the deck, and we enjoyed an explosion of color each year on our deck.

The Store

One of our most interesting and fun challenges was the establishment of our store. It started out with T-shirts and fish bait. Our first year, we had some rather cheap shirts printed in Indianapolis and sold a few. I also knew we needed to offer live bait and initially tried to offer worms, leeches, and minnows. I soon learned that trying to keep minnows alive was difficult and costly, and after one year, ended that effort. I would buy nightcrawlers by the flat (500 worms) and leeches by the pound and then repackage them offering cups with either a dozen worms or a dozen leeches. We kept them fresh in an old refrigerator from Kathie's mom. Leeches were interesting bait. Many guests refused to use them, thinking they would "suck their blood," while they were an excellent choice when fishing for walleyes or bass.

When the addition was finished, we were able to expand our selection of items. We had added postcards, candy, and a much larger selection of T-shirts and sweatshirts. Most had our logo embroidered on them.

We bought most of the clothing from a business in Ely. At one of the sport shows, we met a man selling "machine-carved" wooden ducks, Bundy Ducks. They were the most expensive items in the store. I also started making bird feeders and birdhouses out of gourds. I would paint scenes on the gourds, and they became popular items. We ordered our gourds from Mississippi. During the winter, it was a fun project, and I always took pride in my work whenever one sold.

We always enjoyed interacting with our guests as they browsed through the items in the store. Bait sales were the most active item and Bob's T-shirt the most popular clothing item. For a while, we even offered milk, eggs, and bread, but they never produced much activity.

Mike and Amanda

While all of this was going on, Mike asked if he could bring his girlfriend, Amanda, to the resort for a quick visit over Easter. The day they arrived, it was cold, dripping rain, and we still had patches of snow under the pine trees. I'll never forget her arrival. She hopped out of the car and immediately scurried around hiding items in the snow. She then asked us to find what she'd hidden. When I found the Easter eggs, she seemed perplexed that I could have found them so quickly. I pointed to her footprints in the snow! They did announce that they were planning their wedding, which would be that spring. It's tough to accept, but we told Mike that if that was what he wanted, we would support him 100 percent.

A couple of weeks after they left, Mike informed us that they'd picked a wedding date. It turned out to be the opening day of fishing season in Minnesota, the day we opened the resort for business. Mike wanted Audie to sing at the wedding, and he and Carol agreed to ride with us back to Indy for the wedding. We asked our friends, the Goodman's, to come up and oversee the resort for the days we would be gone. Fortunately, it was a slow business time for the resort.

The Wedding

Audie, Carol, Kathie, and I arrived a couple of days before the wedding. Mike seemed to be in a daze. Amanda had him running around in circles trying to make sure she had the perfect wedding. When we tried to talk with him, he just told us what we were to do and abruptly ended the conversation. The wedding would take place on a set at the local Christian TV station. The happy couple would then ride in a horse-drawn carriage to the reception site some three miles away. The hall had a balcony for the wedding party that overlooked the main floor where the guests would be seated to enjoy a full sit-down dinner. Mike wanted Audie to sing the Lord's Prayer, but when he met with the group playing at the wedding/reception, no music was available.

They had hired a wedding planner whom we later decided had recently retired from the police force. We each received a list of instructions to include a precise wedding schedule. For some reason, I had the job of obtaining the wedding party's tuxes plus the groom's tux. Jim would be the Best Man and Kim was also in the wedding party. We also learned for the first time that the ceremony would be a combined Christian/Jewish wedding. It turned out that Amanda thought of herself as a Messianic Jew. I confess I had never heard the term. Followers apparently believe that Jesus taught and reaffirmed the Torah. There would be two pastors. An Assembly of God man from the church Mike was attending plus a Jewish rabbi. Vows would be said twice and the ritual of the bride circling the groom seven times and then the two of them breaking a wine glass while saying "mazel tov" would be part of the wedding. Mike remained silent on everything while we decided that our only choice was to go along and support him. They also wanted an arch which was again our responsibility to locate, rent and bring to the studio.

Audie and I started the search for his music. It turned into quite a challenge, but we finally found it at a Christian bookstore in Plainfield. Audie loved Mike dearly and I felt sorry for him trying to rehearse in the car as we returned to the south side of Indianapolis. Kathie located an arch at a local party store, and we felt good that all was under control. Next would be the rehearsal and the rehearsal dinner.

Before the rehearsal, Mike and Amanda stopped by Jim's house where we were staying. Other friends were arriving for the wedding and were also at the house. One dear lady, Ursal Pussel, Kathie's second "mom," asked Amanda to come in to meet everyone and she refused, remaining in the car. Poor Urs was crushed, Kathie hurt, and I was upset.

Our schedule included a time for the rehearsal but when we showed up at the studio, the planner met us with, "well the Rusks have finally arrived." The time had been moved up, but no one told us. Part of the set was a spiral staircase where Amanda would be when the ceremony started. When the spotlight came on, she would make her entrance, coming down the staircase. Amazing! We got through the evening, but again, Mike remained silent throughout. He was not happy, and at times I thought he had the look of a "deer in the headlights." Our hearts were sad, but events had overtaken everything. We were then told the studio was short on chairs and because I had a van it was our task to pick up extra chairs for the event. Some planner!

My first task on the morning of the wedding was to pick up the tuxes. Fortunately, everything was ready, and I left the rental business feeling that I had accomplished one task. Little did I know that I'd made a grievous error. Per instructions of our planner, we all met at the studio to change. Mike had selected a little boy from one of his classes to be the ring bearer. He was cute as a button in his little tux. His only problem was that he was black, which caused Amanda to completely ignore him. Mike's tux was white with long tails. His shoes were also white and when he went to put them on, my error came to light. His shoes were size 9 rather than the 13 we had ordered. My assumption that all was correct was terribly wrong. Kathie suggested to Amanda that Mike skip wearing the shoes as his feet would be hidden by her dress. She refused saying that if that was what I had gotten him that was what he would wear. The rental store was closed preventing a quick return. Somehow Mike wore those shoes during the ceremony.

Once we were all dressed, our planner informed us that the groom's family and close friends were to wait in a room until it was time for the ceremony. It was a small room and reminded us of the viewing room at a mortuary! Time went by, and suddenly the door flew open with the planner yelling at us to hurry. She had forgotten that we had been closeted away. When we entered the studio, the bride's side was full while our side was almost empty. We asked if Kathie's cousin could join us near the front, but again the planner would not allow it. What a strange scene. The wedding went well, and Audie did a wonderful job singing the Lord's Prayer.

We then had a receiving line as folks left for the reception. Kathie ended up standing next to Amanda, introducing our side of the family. Amanda remained aloof and simply shook people's hands. She completely ignored the ring bearer's family. In the middle of all of this, my aunt Marigold appeared in line. We had no idea she was coming, as Mike had never shared the guest list with us. Instead of being treated as part of the family, she had been totally ignored, much to my dismay. Both Kathie and I stumbled all over ourselves trying to explain what happened, even though we couldn't. Marigold never communicated with me again since that fateful day.

I know this will sound bad, but the funniest part of the entire event was the horse pulling the carriage peed all over the place as they were leaving, much to Amanda's disdain. While the carriage was making its way to the reception site, we loaded up the arch and returned it to the party shop. When we arrived at the reception, after everyone else had arrived, we discovered that no place had been reserved for the groom's parents. All the tables were full, but the staff managed to squeeze us into a table with folks we had never met before. Throughout the entire reception, Amanda remained above the fray in her balcony seat, staring down at the group. Not exactly the picture of a happy bride. Our hearts went out to Mike as he tried to mingle with everyone while she watched from above.

Finally, the reception was over and everyone on the Rusk side retired to Jim's house to replay the wedding. In the middle of all of this, we received a call from Mike asking that we find Amanda's makeup bag and bring it to the airport motel. Jim made the delivery. Mike and his new bride flew off to Hawaii for a two-week honeymoon the next morning.

The next day, Kim graduated from IUPUI, which we all celebrated in grand fashion. Her graduation was the one highlight of the weekend.

Looking back, we knew we were sad because we knew the marriage would not work. Mike was at a vulnerable stage. His friends were getting married, and he wanted so much to be loved and wanted. We felt Amanda had taken advantage of his plight and events later would prove us to be correct. She made no excuses for the fact that she wanted the wedding of her life and that her "biological" clock was "ticking." Mike spent his entire inheritance from Hilda for the wedding.

The Resort

Our year was very successful. Our guests loved the new

addition. The weekly cookouts were much easier, and everyone enjoyed our deck. We also purchased new docks. The original docks were aging sections of 2 x 4's which we floated out and then flipped over, placing the pipe legs on concrete blocks. They were already old, and we continually struggled with legs that broke after rusting through, slats that broke from being rotten, etc. They were "accidents waiting to happen." Our friend, Bob Koschak, built heavy-duty docks as his main business. We contracted with him for three new docks. They were single-piece docks with wheels which would allow us to pull them out of the lake each winter. The dock for the beach was what I called the "T" dock and looked like an airplane when it was out of the water. In the early years, we had boats sink on the beach when overnight winds would fill the boats with water as the waves crashed onto the beach. The "T" was designed to take the force of the waves and protect our boats. The new docks were again loved by our guests.

I think one key to our success was a decision made early on to replace items that broke with new equipment. If the refrigerator went down, we bought a new one. The mattresses we inherited were broken down, so they were all replaced. Each year, we targeted certain items for replacement within our budget so over our first ten years, improvements could be seen each year. We invested in new boats and motors, buying 16 foot boats to replace our aging fleet of 14 foot boats. I felt this was critical to maintaining our base of repeat customers while also modestly increasing prices each year. The tactic obviously worked as our base of repeat customers remained solid for the years we owned the resort.

New Cabins

Now that we would no longer be returning to Indianapolis each winter, we started discussing the possibility of building new cabins. There was a nice point of land behind our house, and I sketched out how we could build a loop road and place two cabins on the side of the hill overlooking the river. The design was for two-story cabins built into the hill so that they could be entered on the second floor as well as the first. The slope was ideal for such a design. We also knew that our shallow well could not provide adequate water for the new cabins so drilling a deep water well was also included in the plans.

We were about ready to make the final payment on the extra land which would clear the way for assuming new debt. The manager of Norwest Bank was a fellow Rotarian and I approached him with the idea. He outlined what I would need to secure a loan to include the development of a business plan, etc. I felt fortunate to have his assistance, which is a hidden benefit of any service organization, the ability to network with local business leaders. Banks were notorious for not wanting to lend money to resort businesses. The failure rate of our industry was very high, which prompted this reluctance. Therefore, even with the manager's personal support, I wasn't sure until the very end that my request would be granted. When the loan was processed for $125,000, the manager told me that it was only granted because I had my Army retirement. The bank also would not give me the money outright, requiring my contractors to submit bills to the bank for payment.

We hired Jeff Schulze ,the owner of Timber Wolf Lodge, to build the road and contracted with a well driller. Work started in the spring on the well. What a nervous time that was. The driller could care less how deep the well was as he was paid a flat fee for each foot drilled. For two days, we listened to the drilling and saw dollars floating away. At 350 feet, we hit some water but the flow, measured in gallons per minute, was less than one per minute. Certainly not enough for our needs. The driller said they could drill deeper or try to hydrofrack the well. In the old days, there were many stories of drillers dropping dynamite down a well to increase the water flow. That was like me shooting the pistol down our sand point well. The concept of hydrofracking was similar. They used water under extremely high pressure. The effort would add another $3,000 to our bill without any guarantee of success. I opted to hydrofrack. It was quite a process as water was pumped out of the lake, pressurized in a large truck, and then forced into the well. Fortunately, it was the right decision as once the process was finished our water flow increased to 8-10 gallons per minute. More than enough to meet the needs of the entire resort. We were in business.

We then hired a guy with a backhoe to trench from the well down the side of the hill to the well pit down by the lake. The trench had to be seven feet deep to prevent freezing during the winter. It was something to watch the backhoe "hanging" on the side of the hill as the work was done. A plumber then ran plastic pipe from the well to the pit, hooking it to our existing water system and we all enjoyed new well water for the first time. Our shallow lake well was never used again.

The septic systems for the two cabins used a combined drain field located between the two cabins. The hillside was almost totally gravel which made the location ideal for a drain field.

We had also been working with Bob Pinckney, a local builder. He would act as the general contractor and be responsible for all the subcontractors, i.e., electricians, plumbers, etc. Again, our luck held as Bob turned out to be great. I had also taken the liberty of accepting reservations for the new three-bedroom cabins before they were even built. Guests would start arriving on July 15.

It was an incredibly busy time. The original five cabins were occupied, and guests had to be cared for. We took on the task of finding furniture, free-standing fireplaces, plus window treatments, pots and pans and a myriad of other items for each cabin. The interior of the cabins was a combination of drywall and knotty pine paneling. It was also our job to paint both the interior and exterior of each cabin, no small feat. We also had to landscape the area around the cabins and Bob Koschak built stairs to the lake and added a new dock.

Bob Pinckney started work on the cabins the day after Mother's Day, mid-May, and somehow completed the work in under 60 days. What a miracle! On a couple of occasions, I told him that if we were not ready by the 15th, my guests were going to spend their week in his home! We were thrilled when Saturday, July 15 arrived because we could quit working our 18-hour days and relax. Our guests loved the cabins, and we knew that we'd made the right decision. The extra money generated by them would prove to be sufficient to meet the payment requirement on our ten-year loan.

With the new cabins, we also entered a new phase in our business, winter operations. The new cabins had fireplaces, good, forced air heating, and great insulation. We started exploring new advertising outlets plus added our resort to the list of winter places maintained by the Chamber of Commerce.

It also became obvious that Kathie and I would not be able to handle changing over seven cabins each week. Doing the five for all these years had stretched us to absolute maximum. We would need to hire staff first.

Mike Walker

We decided that we needed one full-time employee, five days a week, plus someone to help with the cleaning on Saturdays. At the time, it was relatively easy to find someone for the Saturday work, but I wasn't sure where to look for our full-time employee. Talking it over with Bob Koschak, he recommended Mike Walker, a young man who had worked for him. Mike turned out to be a 15-year-old friend of Bob's son. He had worked at times with Bob, helping him build docks. We agreed to talk with Mike, and one day his dad drove in with Mike. It turned out that Mike was part of a local family with twelve children. His dad had retired from the Army and had been with the Army Air Corps in World War II. He was a slightly built kid but bubbling with enthusiasm. It was an easy decision to hire him. For that first year, his dad would bring him to work each day and pick him up each evening. While our two sons were in Indianapolis, Kathie had another "son" to care for! Mike continued to work for us for several years, and we remain good friends. During the workweek, Mike would join us for lunch. He loved macaroni and cheese, and we would watch as he prepared this dish. Living with twelve brothers and sisters, he was very good at preparing meals for himself.

Mike was also interested in our new guests each week, especially if the family included a teenage girl. One family with such a daughter "adopted" Mike during the week of their visit, inviting him to dinner and other activities. A few years later, Mike and the daughter, Brenda, were married.

Mike and Amanda

Once October rolled around, things became very peaceful at the resort. Business was reduced to maybe a weekend for grouse hunters, and one year we even had a group of moose hunters. It was our time to relax and await the arrival of snow. One evening, we got a call from Amanda that she and Mike had been in an accident. Details were sketchy, but I guess they were arguing as they were traveling along the Interstate in a construction zone, and Mike lost control of the vehicle. They flew through the air, landing upright on the side of a hill. A great deal of damage was done to the car, but no serious injuries to either one of them.

This was our first indication that there was "trouble in paradise." While I know little of the details, things continued to go downhill in their relationship. Mike was not communicating with us but did share some things with Jim. Things finally came to a head in November, and Jim agreed to let Mike move in with him. We were not surprised and in some ways were relieved but very concerned about Mike's mental well-being. We knew that the failure of his marriage would devastate his self-confidence. As I mentioned already, his recovery was measured in gaining new higher plateaus. We knew these events would cause him to drop to a lower plateau.

Our concerns were brought to a head over Christmas. Mike drove up to join us and quite frankly it was a "Christmas from Hell." He was quiet from the beginning, not responding to questions and when he did talk, he would lash out at us. He had no other place to dump his frustrations but upon us. It hurt a great deal but at least we understood what was causing everything.

Mike was also concerned about money. His job was not high-paying and while he had plans to return to college, money for living expenses, etc., was very tight. He did have several shares of stock in a utility, Southern Company. I had gotten both him and Jim 100 shares in the late 1970s and Mike had added dollars to the account and reinvested the dividends for several years. We discussed how much he needed, and I suggested that he sell a few shares and use the money to move forward with his plans. It proved to be an excellent suggestion and allowed Mike to move forward.

Later the next year, Mike and Amanda got a simple no-contest divorce. Amanda did one good thing by allowing the divorce to proceed quietly. Mike fought the idea of divorce for a while but finally realized that it what had to be done. I have no idea what happened to Amanda. At last word she was still using the Rusk name.

1993-2000

These years were basically routine. So, rather than try to proceed year by year, I will cover events, situations, etc. When a specific time frame is needed, I will add them where appropriate. Our entire focus during this time was to grow the business.

Resort Support Group

Our business kept us from really getting involved in the communities of Ely and Babbitt. The folks we did get to know were usually associated with our business. Such an association led to the creation of the Resort Support Group.

The group consisted of four resort owners: ourselves;

Lori and Jeff Schulze, owners of Timber Wolf Lodge; Gary and Barb Detoffel, owners of Olson Bay Resort; and Heather and Fitz Fitzgerald, owners of Northernaire Resort. We found that we enjoyed each other's company and started to use whatever excuse we could to get together in the off-season. We met at one of our places to celebrate birthdays, holidays, the end of the season, the start of a new season, or whatever. While we were in competition with each other, we all understood that we all needed to work together to make our operations more attractive. Over time, we ended up sharing employees and jointly supporting various issues before the Chamber of Commerce while having great fun together.

I think the best part was just sharing our experiences with the businesses. We all had maintenance problems and, more importantly, guest problems. Our philosophies about how to treat customers were varied, but we enjoyed many good laughs talking about our problems. The group began to fall apart when Heather and Fitz sold their resort. They ended up leaving the area for several years to work other jobs. We continued getting together and became very good friends with Barb and Gary and Jeff and Lori.

Barb and Gary were an interesting pair. Gary told us that he'd been a lawyer specializing in union negotiations prior to buying Olsen Bay. Their resort had about 10 cabins plus a restaurant and had been in business for 40-plus years. During the first years of their ownership, things went well. Then Gary started having health problems (heart/stroke) and things started to change. He suddenly became quite aggressive and abusive at the bar in the restaurant. This started an agonizing spiral downhill for both. Over time, complaints about the restaurant and cabins grew, and business dropped. This reduced the cash flow and reduced their ability to make needed upgrades. It also increased the tension between them. We had a wonderful wedding reception at their place in 1997, but their operation continued to deteriorate. They did manage to sell before going bankrupt but gained little from the sale due to their debt load. They left for Barb's hometown, Myrtle Beach, SC to work. However, they divorced, and shortly thereafter Gary passed away in Texas. A remarkably sad story. We are still in contact with Barb.

Just the opposite was true for Jeff and Lori. Over the years, we became very close. They had a family of young children when we first met, and Lori had their fourth child, Cody, while they owned the resort. Timber Wolf Lodge was much larger than our place, with a dozen cabins, a campground, and a restaurant. It had also been in operation for 30-plus years and had fallen into hard times when Jeff & Lori took over. They proved to be classic "entrepreneurs," hardworking, willing to take risks, and totally aware of their customer wants. They closed the restaurant and worked hard redoing the cabins, septic systems, grounds, etc. Jeff had experience with earthmoving equipment and used his knowledge to great effect. Before they were finished, they had rebuilt the lodge, added garages, and completely changed the atmosphere of their business. We ended up sharing equipment and guests with each other. In the winter, Jeff helped me with his equipment when the snow got too high and marked snowmobile trails for our guests. Kathie helped Lori in the kitchen when they had special groups needing food service, the only time the restaurant was used. It was a fun, positive relationship which we still enjoy today. They sold the resort a few years before we did and remain in Ely.

Wood Cutting

With the new cabins, plus the new fireplace in our home, the need for good, seasoned firewood became a must. Jim came up with a solution to this need. He asked if he and a couple of his fellow police officer friends could come up and help cut, split, and stack the wood. This turned out to be a wonderful start to our year. The guys would take a week off work and arrive a few days before the opening of fishing. Usually three would come: Jim, Tom, and Bill, and on occasion a fourth. If Mike Walker wasn't in school, he would also help. Mike loved to work with the guys and was in awe of their "police stories." In the first couple of years, we concentrated on dead trees lining our road. We would cut the tree, chunk it into 5 – 6 foot lengths, carry it to the truck and then back to the resort. It was long, hard work. We always seemed to be sharpening a chainsaw chain or whatever to keep the work going. When we had collected sufficient wood, I rented a gas-powered splitter, and the wood was cut into smaller pieces and split. Another back-breaking process. The fireplaces in the cabins were smaller than those in the house, so two different lengths had to be cut. The final step was stacking the wood either near the house or near the cabins so that it could "cure" throughout the summer. We then ended their visit with fishing trips on Bear Island Lake and on occasion a trip up to Basswood Lake.

Once we'd cleared out the dead trees, I would buy ten cords of wood. The cords were delivered in "loggers" length, eight feet long. It always proved to be amazing how many 24 inch pieces were in ten cords. This system worked for about seven years.

Kathie and I really loved the camaraderie of the guys. It was great fun to banter back and forth with them, and Kathie loved to fix good meals, which they really appreciated. Jim and Tom worked together on the police force until Jim's retirement in 2023.

Guiding

On occasion, our guests would ask for a guide. Over the years, I had two professional guides work for us, but they had both moved on to other occupations. I would offer myself as a guide and quickly learned that it was no easy task. When guests were paying for the service, they expected results, so the pressure to produce fish was immediately on my shoulders. For the most part, I was able to make our trips a fun event with fish in the boat. I always said a silent prayer when we caught the first keeper!

One trip will always stand out in my memory. Two men asked if I could guide them into Basswood Lake, and they wanted to fish on the Canadian side of the lake. I found another guide, Andy Hill, in Ely who specialized in fishing Basswood. We had to use canoes to fish in Canada, so we decided to use two square stern canoes with three horsepower motors. We used the motors to take us up the Moose Lake chain to Prairie Portage and after arriving on Basswood went through Canadian customs located near the portage. We then had to paddle as motors were not permitted in Canadian waters. We ended up fishing near one of the many islands and had good success catching walleyes and bass. As we were fishing, we noticed three canoes heading our way. They were following a zig-zag course which meant they were new to the sport of canoeing. When they reached us, it was three couples, and they asked directions to an island where their overnight campsite was located. We were able to point them in the right direction, and as they headed out, one of the women said, "and to think we have to pay to do this." A good laugh.

On our way back, we encountered a raging thunderstorm. As the wind rose, the waves became higher, threatening to swamp the canoe. My guest had been asleep in the front of the canoe, and I got him awake and into his life vest. Our only option was to head near shore and keep the bow pointed into the waves and hope the motor would not quit. The storm passed, and we headed on to the landing. As we approached, we noticed a "cloud" near the launch ramp. When we arrived, the cloud turned out to be huge swarms of mosquitoes. We swatted bugs as we loaded the canoes on the trailer, and I couldn't help but think about the three couples camping in rain and the mosquitoes.

While I enjoyed fishing with our guests and getting to know them better, I was happy that I was not trying to make my living by guiding.

Canoe Trips

We had 4 canoes and would, on occasion, rent them to our guests. For many, it was their first time in a canoe, and we saw a few folks capsize them as they attempted to board standing up. We also offered short trips to other lakes in the area. I had a canoe trailer, and we would load the canoes, gear, and people into the truck and drop them off at a lake. We would set a time for pick up, and I'd return and bring everyone back to the resort. There were three small lakes that could produce good fishing: Sock, Whisper, and Perch Lake were popular destinations. Folks could also take the canoes down Bear Island River from our boathouse to Highway 21, about five miles away. The river wound through the woods and even had a short portage around some rapids. Pike, bass, and panfish were available, and the trips proved to be a popular half-day wilderness adventure. Again, I would take the trailer down to the bridge on Highway 21 to pick up our guests.

Chamber and Rotary

The business consumed almost all our time, and it was difficult to make friends locally other than our Resort Support Group and Audie and Carol. Kathie, a member of the sewing club in Babbitt, made many good friends through that outlet.

I decided to get heavily involved with Rotary and the Ely Chamber of Commerce. Early on, I'd been involved with the Babbitt Chamber, even serving as its President. However, that organization was pretty much ineffective because the "city fathers" did not support tourism. This factor turned me towards Ely. While it was called a Chamber of Commerce, the organization was more like a Tourism Bureau. It did have shop owners, but again the emphasis was on luring customers into the stores versus attracting businesses to Ely, a traditional Chamber role. I was elected to the Board of Directors and spent one year as the Chamber President. I enjoyed being involved with the organization and contributed many hours to its operation during the winter months.

Ely had a 3 percent lodging tax which all resorts added to our guests' bills. The monies generated from the tax were required by law to be used in promoting the area. A separate board, the Lodging Tax Board, had the task of administering these monies. Again, I got involved and served a couple of years as the Board President. Annually, the tax would raise about $100,000, and many spirited debates were held among the board members on how to use the dollars for effective advertising. Just like our business, deciding how and where to get the most "bang for the buck" in advertising was and remained a major challenge.

When I first joined the Ely Rotary Club, I wasn't too impressed. It was more of a social club than a service club. Its biggest fundraiser was a club auction of "gag" gifts. In those days, members were expected to spend $100 for "nothing," and back then that was a great deal of money to a struggling business owner. The complexion of the club changed as time went on.

Rotary was finally allowing women to join, and our first women members brought a renewed sense of service to the club. Our first female Rotarian was Jeannie Larson, the owner of the local radio station. She was the same lady I'd spent that first Sport Show with back in 1982. One year the club came up with the idea of a radio auction to raise money. Club members would solicit donations from our local businesses, resorts, and outfitters, and then we would auction the items off during the day that the club "took over" the radio station.

Some of us were on the radio while other members manned the phones and passed the bids to those on the radio. Each hour we would offer a new batch of items and close out the sales for the previous hour's work. Quite a hectic day but as time passed, we became more efficient with the help of computer programs which allowed those on the radio to see current bids and urge the community to run the bid up. Items varied from gift certificates to restaurants to guided fishing trips to ten yards of black dirt. Over the years, businesses saw what the club did for the community, and it became easier to solicit good auction items. One of the first contributions to the community was the purchase of a portable defibrillator for our local first responders. The auction continues to be the major fundraiser for the club today. It was good positive feedback to work on a project and then see the results benefit the community.

I continue to enjoy Rotary today.

The Chamber Executive Director, Linda Fryer, and I became close friends during my stints on the Chamber and Lodging Tax boards. She was a great fisherperson, and we spent many days fishing together on Basswood Lake. Usually, three or four of us would take Linda's boat to Fall Lake and portage it into Basswood. She had a set of portage wheels, but it was still back-breaking labor dragging the boat across two portages into Basswood. Fortunately, good fishing was our reward, which made the return trip across the portage easier. Linda remained Executive Director for several years and had that special quality of being able to help members overcome their personal differences for the benefit of everyone.

Gasoline

When we purchased the resort, it had a 500 gallon underground gas tank. I loved its convenience and used it for our vehicles and the outboard motors. Normally, I would only keep about 200-300 gallons in the tank, and I kept a log on what was used so that I could reorder before we ran out. In spring 1995, I noticed that the tank seemed to be running out quicker than my log said it should. I also noticed some gasoline sheen on rain puddles down by the fish cleaning house. Initially, I wrote it off to poor bookkeeping. However, one day a guest mentioned that they thought they'd smelled gasoline, so I became concerned the tank was leaking.

Not knowing what to do, I made the decision to inform the Minnesota Environmental Protection Agency (EPA). This notification started a huge chain of events that would take over two years to resolve. There were many times during the process that I regretted deciding to play "by the rules." There were also times that I feared this leak could result in our bankruptcy.

The EPA required that the tank be removed, the soil around the tank removed and tested and treated and then finally a series of tests on the groundwater. There was a federal cleanup fund which could pay up to 90 percent of these costs. There were lists of approved contractors to do the work and we had to "up front" the cost and then hope for reimbursement. I selected a guy who was on my list to remove the tank and hired a testing firm in Duluth to test the soil and water. When we got the tank out, we found about three pin holes that were the cause of the problem. When I submitted the invoice for reimbursement it was rejected because the EPA said the contractor was not on their list. $3,000 down the drain. Later they said he was on the list and even allowed him to treat the soil, but we never got any reimbursement for the first removal action. Soil tests showed a very low level of contamination, and our next chore was deciding how to clean the soil.

When we reached this stage, contractors came out of the "woodwork" offering their services. Some wanted to put bacteria eating "bugs" into the soil. Others wanted to truck it to Duluth to be burned. Finally, we got approval to simply allow the soil to clean itself by biodegrading. The contractor mixed straw with the soil, covered it with black plastic, and allowed it to sit for the rest of the summer and through the winter. In the spring, the soil tested good, and I used it to fill holes on our road.

The final obstacle was the issue of testing the groundwater. Our testing firm initially submitted a plan to the EPA requiring three test wells to be drilled around the site. Estimated cost: $35,000. I almost had a heart attack. Kathie and I met in Duluth with the company officials to try to find an alternative. Fortunately, our two existing groundwater wells came to our rescue. Based on the facts of the ground hydrology, i.e., sloping downhill to the lake from the site, the company was able to obtain EPA approval to use the water in those wells for testing. The next summer, testing revealed good water and finally in 1997 we got final documentation from the EPA stating that the cleanup of the site was completed. What a relief.

We also had to replace the tank. New EPA rules forbid the use of underground tanks, and I purchased a 300-gallon above-ground tank which proved to work quite well, meeting all our needs.

What an experience and learning experience. Fortunately, the matter was finally resolved satisfactorily but it created a great deal of stress for all of us.

Winter Business

The new cabins were designed for winter business and entering that phase of our operation was a logical step forward. During the summer, I felt that we could control the business using the philosophy of providing good accommodations, personal service, and a positive wilderness experience for our guests. It had worked well for nearly 10 years.

We soon discovered that such a philosophy, while helpful, did not work in the winter. Winter business was at the mercy of Mother Nature. Very frustrating for someone like me. Our main attractions were snowmobiling and cross-country skiing. To be successful, we needed early good snow as well as sufficient cold weather to fully freeze the lake to a safe depth. All things over which we had no control. If we got heavy snow before the lake was fully frozen, the ice could become soft and unsafe. Early on, we discovered what a great insulator snow is. One morning, it was about -40, and there was about two feet of snow on the ground. We walked out on the lake and found that despite the serious cold, there was still a layer of slush on top of the ice. Amazing!

Winter business was also different in that folks tended to make shorter trips, usually weekends. They were also mainly from the Twin Cities (Minneapolis/St. Paul). Both factors were quite different from our summer guests. There were weeks when we had to clean the cabins two or three times each week. There was no way to hire out this work, so it fell upon us. We were able to attract some of our summer guests to visit us in the winter, but for the most part, had to find new customers.

The phone rang continuously with folks asking about weather conditions and snow conditions. We decided early on to provide accurate information, opting not to try to make a sale by stretching the truth. During all our years in the summer business, I could count the number of late cancellations on my fingers. However, cancellations were a fact of life in the winter. We had cancellations when the snowmobile trails were in bad shape due to the lack of snow. We had them when the snow was too deep. We had them when the temperatures dropped to minus 30 or 40. We had them when Minneapolis received a snowstorm preventing folks from traveling north. Such was life for businesses trying to make a buck in the winter.

Usually, our weather problems were associated with the lack of sufficient snow. However, one year - the winter from Hell - the problem was just the opposite. It would not quit snowing, and by January, we were in waist-deep snow. While beautiful, the snow created many problems for us. Our truck had a standard 8 foot blade and simply pushed the snow out of the way. As I have already mentioned, the road was over a half-mile long, not very wide, and bordered by many trees. Over time, the piles of snow would reach so high, six feet or more, that newly plowed snow would simply roll back down on the road. I will never forget the day that Kathie and I plowed the road. With nowhere to put the snow, we would push it about a hundred feet until the pile was about as high as the truck. We then climbed over the snowbank and shoveled the snow in front of the truck into the woods. What a day. We were both ready to drop when we finally reached the highway. Later, I hired Jeff to bring his Bobcat over to lift and push snow deeper into the woods.

That same winter, we had folks scheduled in when a major snowstorm hit. We got the road to the cabins plowed but still had to shovel paths from the road to the cabins. Again, waist deep, taking two or three shovel fills to proceed. Kathie got stuck above her waist, and I had to dig her out. While it was a good laugh, it was also back-breaking work. Finally, the work was finished, we crawled back into the truck and returned home. When we got inside, there was a message waiting for us. Our customers had canceled because of the heavy snow! Such was winter business.

Deep snow also created many problems during the spring. Starting in late March and running through April, we had warmer days causing the snow to melt and cold nights which re-froze the melt-off. The surface of the road was snow-covered and would turn into a sheet of ice. There were days when the hill beside the house was so frozen, we were unable to climb it with a car. Fortunately, I discovered that spreading ashes from the fireplaces solved the problem.

One spring, we encountered an entirely new problem.

Our road crossed a small creek. It ran through a small culvert below the road, which would freeze solid during the winter. As the snow began to melt, water would flow over the road until the culvert finally thawed. During normal snow years, this process would take a couple of weeks, but the water would never get over a few inches deep. This one year, the snow was very heavy, and the water flowed well over a foot deep and was some twenty yards wide. Going back and forth, our truck rutted the road, and due to very cold nights, the ruts would freeze solid, and the layer of ice covering the road continued to get deeper. What a mess.

We still had guests and spent days trying to make sure they could safely cross this stretch of road. We laid wood planks and then spent hours chipping at the ice to allow the water to drain. It was so bad I had to leave our Escort parked on the other side of the creek and walk into the resort. Things finally came to a head when our four-wheel drive truck got stuck. It bottomed out on the ice, and the four tires simply spun. Jeff brought his backhoe over and literally had to pick the truck up so it could be moved. We finally solved the problem by hiring Jeff's brother and another guy, and all of us hand-chipped the ice off the road. Fortunately, it only happened that one year. Never a dull moment in resort life.

The Indianapolis Sport Show also created a new situation. February was probably the busiest month in the winter. Snow was at its highest, and the temperatures were starting to moderate. Our decision was to remain open. Kathie would go to Indy to do the show while I remained at home taking care of business. For the most part, things went well. I gained a deep appreciation of all the work Kathie had done over the years as I struggled trying to clean the bathrooms and kitchens when a cabin turned over. My biggest concern was Kathie driving alone between Ely and Indianapolis. She was able to make the trip, but you never knew what she would encounter. One year, a snowstorm was coming, and we agonized over whether Kathie should leave. We finally decided for her to go, and it turned into quite a trip. The snowstorm hit Duluth, and Kathie found herself watching car after car slide into snowdrifts as she made her way south through Wisconsin. Somehow, she made it without incident, another testimony to her grit and toughness. Jim was shocked that we didn't own a cell phone and bought one for his mom before she made the return trip home.

Those trips were a lonely time for me. Kathie would always prepare my meals and freeze them ahead of time, but the place got very still when no one was around. I began to understand what Jim had gone through all those months we were in Florida with Mike. One night, I was plowing in the middle of a storm when suddenly there was a loud bang in the front of the truck, and I plowed directly into a snowbank. When I got out of the truck, there were pieces of gears from the 4-wheel drive all over the road. I managed to walk over to Jeff's at Timber Wolf Lodge, and finally, after much digging, we were able to get the truck to his place. It was even lonelier when I didn't have a vehicle to use!

Looking back, while we really had no choice but to remain open in the winter, we never generated much money. I think maybe $5,000 was the most we ever grossed all winter, which is what we did in a good week during the summer. As we got older, fighting the snow and cold also became more difficult. In our last years, I hired Jeff to do much of the plowing to help ease the burden of winter business.

2-1/2 Acres

If you remember back, when we bought the extra land, I mentioned that included everything but five acres. The story at the time was that Fred had promised the land to the church. My problem was that the land cut through our road. On numerous occasions I would offer to buy the land, but they always refused. His wife even told me that "Hell would freeze over" before they sold us the property. One day in the mid-1990s, I found a couple of trucks parked on the road. It turned out to be Fred's partner John and another guy. John told me they were selling the land to the other man and were discussing building sites. Again, something that I did not want to happen. Something had to be done without them knowing I was involved. Enter our friends Jeff and Lori. The land abutted their property, and I asked Jeff to find out what was happening.

Sure enough, the sale was going on. It turned out that the other party involved had business dealings with them, and the sale was sort of a repayment of a debt of some sort. Jeff found out the selling price and we "hatched" a plan. Once the sale was complete, Jeff would offer the guy $5,000 more than what he had paid. Knowing that money would "talk" with him. Jeff would then sell the half to me that contained our road. I agreed to pay all the closing costs and sure enough the deals went through, and we took possession of our land. To celebrate we put up a road sign on Highway 21, "Rusk's Road" to let everyone know that "Hell had frozen over!" Two and a half acres more for the resort and many, many worries solved. It was a good day.

Colton John

In late fall 1995, we received word from Jim that Kim was pregnant. The birth was scheduled for July 1996. What wonderful news. They had waited nearly ten years then had a great deal of difficulty becoming pregnant. Two sessions of in vitro fertilization were needed for the great event to happen. It was a happy time and Kathie was even able to be with Kim for one of her checkups during the 1996 Sport Show trip where the sonogram showed that we were having a grandson. Everything went well except for a brief scare when a technician overreacted to an amniocentesis test.

Colton would be our first grandchild and we wanted very much to be part of his birth. We talked with Heather and Fitz who had just sold their resort and they agreed to step in and run our place while we went to Indy after his birth.

On the morning of July 19, Jim called saying that Kim was in labor and that he would call with updates. In the mid-afternoon he called again saying that the head was almost out, and he would call back shortly. Then nothing! Some two hours after that last call, Kathie was frantic with worry thinking something had happened and that something was preventing Jim from calling. About 5 p.m., a Babbitt police car drove into the resort. A very rare occurrence. The officer asked for us and told us he had a message from Jim. Colton John had been born without complications but when he tried to call the phone was out of service. We checked and sure enough, our phone had not been placed properly back into its receiver. Guests had used the phone that afternoon, so I guess that was where the mistake was made. The visit also made the police blotter printed in the Babbitt Weekly newspaper, so Colton was a celebrity the day he was born!

We left that evening for Indy and were able to spend a week with Jim and Kim helping them to get settled with the new baby. He did have a little jaundice which required him to spend a few nights in a light chamber and we gave him the nickname "little lighting bug."

When Jim and Kim visited it was always a joy to be with the grandkids. I was able to watch Colton catch his first fish which brought back so many memories of when his dad and Mike were growing up and I taught them how to fish. A treasured photo is one of Jim and Colton fishing off a dock at the resort.

Mike & Jill

As I've mentioned earlier, Mike went through quite a down period after his divorce from Amanda. However, he changed jobs, becoming a Job Trainer for Special Ed kids for the Indianapolis Public School system. He was also working towards accumulating credits towards obtaining his teaching certificate in Special Education. We exchanged letters and phone calls and suddenly Mike began to tell us that he and his "friend" had done this or that. We had no idea who the friend was, and Mike said nothing more than his friend. During the

1996 Sport Show, Mike had bought a house and was moving from his apartment on the IUPUI campus. The move was a family event and one of the movers was Mike's friend, Jill Stewart. Jill was working at an adult rehabilitation center and had met Mike at a meeting. The story of how they got together is quite interesting. But it's their story and not mine so will let them tell it in their own way. The important thing was that Kathie immediately saw how much Jill made Mike happy and we were thrilled that, just maybe, Mike had found the love of his life.

When the Christmas holiday season rolled around, Mike asked if he and Jill could spend the holidays with us. It was a wonderful time. I think one of the cabins was rented but we were basically all to ourselves. Mike told us that it was his intention to propose to Jill during their visit. We offered him my mom's engagement ring which he happily accepted. One morning, he asked her to take a walk with him through the resort. She was getting ready and to Mike it seemed like it was taking her forever. Then they had to put on all the boots and jackets before the trip. They finally headed down towards Cabin 4 where Jim and Kim had been married and when they returned, they were engaged. What a wonderful event and what a wonderful scene to see Mike happy. Something we had not seen for many years.

For Christmas we went out and cut a tree and decorated it with outside lights, etc. It is a Rusk tradition to have our Christmas-on-Christmas morning. Before retiring on Christmas Eve, I told them they were not allowed out of their room until the "rooster crowed." We had a magnetic rooster on the refrigerator that crowed when you pushed it. The next morning, we could hear them both in the room but as instructed they waited for the rooster! Great times.

Before they left, they asked if they could be married on the lake and selected May 28 as the date. Thanks to Jim and Kim's wedding we knew what to do and resolved that we'd make it as special as we could for them.

The Wedding

As the end of May approached, Mother Nature seemed to want to play a role in the wedding. We had a large amount of snow that year, and winter just kept hanging on. We were located on the south edge of the lake, and snow was the last to leave on the south side. Plus, the area for the wedding was tucked into a little cove and on the 25th we still had a foot of snow. We kept telling the kids about the snow, but I really don't think they believed us.

After struggling to carry the organ down and up from there for Jim's wedding, we opted to use "canned" music instead. Finally, on the 26th the snow left, but things remained mushy, and when the snow leaves in the spring, it is replaced with many hungry insects! Jim was scheduled to be the Best Man but just before the three of them were to head north, Colton became quite ill, and they had to cancel the trip. I agreed to fill in as Best Man. The group was smaller than Jim and Kim's wedding, but Jill had almost everyone from her side including her aunt from Alaska, which was nice. My brother's ex-wife, Harriet, and her daughter Jennifer also flew in from DC for the event. Jeff and Lori agreed to open the restaurant for our rehearsal dinner, and we contracted with Barb and Gary to have the reception at their resort. We also reserved rooms for Mike and Jill at another resort nearby. As a special event, I contracted with a local air service to fly the newlyweds from our place to the reception at Olson Bay.

The wedding itself went off without a hitch and was quite funny. Jill had a pug and a chihuahua, and both sported a garter around their necks. In the middle of the service, the chihuahua came down the steps, sat next to Jill, and started scratching the garter. It made the garter spin around its neck, and everyone burst into laughter. Everyone also got a good laugh out of Jill's shoes. They had been dyed to match her dress, but as she stood on the damp ground, the dye slowly drained away and she ended up with two-tone shoes by the time they were declared "Man and Wife." We had the plane timed to land after the wedding, but he was a few minutes late. Fitz had volunteered to be the photographer, and I got him to take every conceivable picture of the wedding group, hoping the plane would arrive. Just as Fitz was running out of ideas, the plane arrived. Mike was so funny. As it circled to land, we all watched and then after landing it taxied across the lake to our dock. He had no idea it was coming for him. After tying up, the pilot hopped out with a string of Just Married balloons. What a sight! Mike's last request was to take Bob along, but of course, we couldn't do that. We all watched the plane race down the lake and take off, quite a unique sendoff. The pilot took them on a brief sightseeing tour on the way to Olson Bay showing Jill where we'd first vacationed when we started coming to Ely.

The reception was great. Everyone was relaxed and had fun. What a great way to welcome Jill into our family.

Corri Rusk

In early 1998, Jim and Kim announced that they were pregnant again. This pregnancy came as quite a shock because after having to go through in vitro, they never imagined they would get pregnant on their own. However, miracles do happen. This one would be named Corri. She was expected in November, which for us was great. We never had business that time of the year, and once we knew about when she'd be born, we stopped taking reservations and headed for Indianapolis. It was a happy time as we all awaited her birth.

One afternoon after a visit to the doctor in the morning, Kim started having labor pains. Jim was at work, so it was agreed that I would take Kim to the hospital. Kathie would stay home with Colton, and Jim would meet us in the hospital. I think Kim was a little disappointed with the plan as she had visions of Jim flying home in his police car, lights flashing, and sirens blaring. Instead, she had to put up with me. I took her to the hospital and settled into a room. Then I was paid a "great" compliment when the doctor invited me to join him to examine Kim as the baby's father. Kim immediately straightened out the doctor, and I made a hasty retreat! Jim soon arrived, and later that evening, Corri was born. For Kathie and me, this was a wonderful time as we were able to participate fully with Corri, while with Colton, we could become involved after the fact.

Our Guests

Probably the most interesting and fun part of all our years in the business was the relationships we built with many of our guests. In the 1990s, we enjoyed almost 60 percent repeat business, and each week was a grand reunion with friends as they returned for their vacations. Some, like the Hashmal's, returned almost every year for 18 years. David was a lawyer with a high-powered firm in Minneapolis, and when they first came, they simply enjoyed the environment, reading, and relaxing. I talked to him about fishing, and finally one year got him to try it. I took him out, teaching him the basics, and before long he was renting a boat/motor and fishing. They had a son one winter, and we babysat to allow them to go out for dinner. The first time they had left the baby. The only year they missed was when their daughter was born. During their last visit before we sold, David and his now 17-year-old son were taking canoe trips together in the Boundary Waters. What fun to watch the family grow over the years.

Another good friend was Barb Zink. She first started coming with her daughter and mom. Her mom was German, and she and Kathie became good friends. As time went by, the mom passed away, but Barb remained a loyal customer throughout. She was a great fisherwoman, and one evening when the fishing was particularly tough, she returned with two large walleyes. I paraded her around to the other cabins to let our guests know that "yes, there are fish in the lake." Fun times and we fished together many times. We are still close and correspond frequently.

Fred Saylor would also come twice a year with his mom. He was a great fisherman and would always catch huge fish, both Northern Pike and Walleyes. He would release everything and at times had to struggle to find a small walleye that he and his mom could enjoy for supper. They were both diehard Kansas City Chief fans and would join us whenever they played on TV. We always got quite a kick out of Mom Saylor in her Chief's sweatshirt cheering them on. I fished many evenings with Fred, and we last saw each other in Indianapolis when he came to enjoy the Brickyard 400. Mom has passed away.

This section wouldn't be complete without talking about Goodman's - Don and Rosemary. They stayed with us first in 1983. Our introduction was her coming into the office with a plastic sandwich bag full of fleas. We learned that the folks in the cabin before them had flea-infested dogs. This unlikely event led us to become good friends. They also visited us in the winter, and one time we decided to snowshoe through the woods to Bear Island River. What an adventure! None of us had experience with the shoes, and we kept falling into the deep snow and then struggling to get up. We made it to the river and then enjoyed warm soup at a local restaurant. Don and Rosemary had honeymooned on Bear Island Lake many years earlier and always dreamed of owning property on the lake. Finally, in the mid-1990s they bought a piece of land across the lake and while we lost them as customers, we have remained great friends to this day. Don was an excellent electrician and helped me wire the screen porches and the new addition when they were built. Later, they built a large home on their property, and we even spent time helping them one fall after we sold the resort. Great friends!

The Goodman's also introduced us to Ruthie Hanson and Ralph Palmer. They were longtime residents of the area and lived side by side on our neighboring lake, Birch. Their properties were right on the lake shore with beautiful views of the lake. Each had unique stories about how they came to the area. Ralph lived in Colorado, divorced, and moved to the area to start a new life. He can best be described as an "almost hermit." One feature that caught your eye as you passed his home was an airplane parked in his garage. His goal over the years was to repair and fly the plane, but it never moved over the years we knew him. Ruthie moved to the area when her husband took a job at the iron ore mine in Babbitt. They started building their home, but he passed just after the basement had been completed, and she lived in her basement for years unable to afford the cost of building "up above" as she called it. She was maybe twenty years older than Kathie, but they became fast friends. During the winter I would plow her driveway and around the house, and Kathie would take her shopping in Ely or Babbitt. It seemed that whenever they went to town, it would snow, and they became known as the "blizzard sisters." We enjoyed many meals and fun times together over the years. When the Goodman's visited during the winter, we shared meals with them and Ruthie. One evening, they left to take Ruthie home and suddenly we saw the car backing down the road. They had encountered a skunk at the top of the hill by the house, a full "stand-off." After three more tries the skunk finally left the road, and Ruthie made it home OK. More good laughs! After we left the area, Ruthie's son finished her home, and she was able to spend her final years "up above" enjoying the wonderful view of Birch Lake. Many other names come to mind as I write this, the McCoy's, the Bachus's plus too many more to list. All good people and the hidden asset of the resort business.

Before I leave the subject must tell one funny story about a "one time" guest. As part of our Tuesday night cookout's, we hired a Naturalist to give programs. They were normally young women that applied for work through the US Forest Service. Most years, we would share the girls' time with the resorts in the Resort Support Group. In our case, the naturalist would talk about some type of animal or bird after the cookout and then return one day during the week to do crafts or a nature hike with the kids in the resort that week. After the cookout, we also did "minnow races" for the kids. I would set up rain gutter tracks, buy a couple dozen minnows, and we'd let the kids' "race" them from one end to the other. Great fun for everyone, which would culminate when we fed the minnows to the bass we had in our fish tank. One week, Cabin 2 had a large family, but they did not come to the cookout. The kids were seen sitting on the steps at the cabin watching what was going on. Finally, during the minnow races one of the kids came over and participated. We asked him why they had missed the cookout. Turns out, the mom and dad thought our naturalist was a nudist and certainly did not want their children to see that. They never came back! Such is life when you deal with people.

Arrows

We also came up with the idea of offering our guests the opportunity to paint an arrow. I cut "arrows" out of 1 x 4 inch pieces of wood, and we provided the paints for them to create an arrow. When completed, I varnished them and then nailed them to trees around the resort. It turned into a fun project for everyone. Each person had their own ideas of what they wanted on the arrow. We had everything from hometowns to wildlife to family names. The new owners continued the project and placed arrows along the road leading into the resort. People often ask what we miss most about leaving the business. One thing is all the friends and loyal customers we enjoyed over the years. Yes, some customers drove us to count the days before they'd leave, but most, the vast majority, were great people.

It was not All work and no Play!

Over the years, we were able to enjoy many fun times. These included special fishing trips, dog sled trips, the real Northern Lights, and just the pure enjoyment of our environment. The prime fishing lake in the area was Basswood Lake located in the Boundary Waters Canoe Area (BWCA). The lake was huge and stretched between the US and Canada. Most of the lake had been designated as "canoe only," but boats/motors were still permitted in parts of the lake. The area was total wilderness and offered great fishing opportunities plus the joy of a true wilderness adventure. In the fall, the crappies would "school" together in preparation for the winter and provided the chance to catch a wonderful eating fish. Business was quiet one year, and Kathie and I decided to make the trip. We even brought along our camp stove and other supplies so that we could have a shore lunch as part of the trip. We obtained a permit and towed the boat to our starting point on Moose Lake and motored to the portage into Basswood Lake.

To reach the lake, we had to have the boat towed across

the portage, about a mile, and then launch it into Basswood. A local resort owner provided the service for a fee. We headed up the lake to a bay known for holding good populations of crappies. There were other boats in the bay, all catching fish, and I was finally able to solve the mystery of how to get them to bite, and together we caught about a dozen fish adding them to the boat's live well. There was a small island, and we pulled ashore to prepare our shore lunch. While I cleaned the fish, Kathie got the stove, etc., set up, and we began preparing our lunch. I had forgotten some supplies and returned to the boat, and there was our boat about to sink. I had forgotten to turn off the pump to the live well, and the water had overflowed into the boat, and it was about an inch away from sinking. After some frantic bailing, the problem was under control. Had the boat sunk, I'm not sure what would have happened. We did enjoy a wonderful shore lunch of freshly caught fried crappies but had many stories to tell when we got home.

During the winter, Basswood Lake and the BWCA offered many opportunities for dog sledding adventures into the wilderness. As I mentioned earlier in my write-up about Dorothy Molter, snowmobiles had been banned from the BWCA, so dog sleds were their only permitted mode of transportation during the winter. My Rotary club had offered a guided day trip by sled dog into the BWCA as part of our annual Rotary

Radio Auction. If items did not receive a bid, the club would hold a "club auction" for the unsold items. One year I was able to purchase the trip for a reasonable price. Our guide was Billy Slaughter, a well-known local outdoorsman. It took a couple of tries to set up the trip as the weather had turned unusually cold. Minus 30 with high winds. Things settled down, and we made the trip on a bright sunny day with the temperature near -10. Kathie and I met Billy at a boat landing on Fall Lake. Our route would take us up the lake and across the four-mile portage into Basswood Lake. He had about sixteen dogs in his trailer and hooked up two sleds, announcing that I was to guide one while he led the way with his team. Billy said all would go well as my team would follow his as we traveled. Once the dogs were in their harnesses, they were "ready to go," and we took off like a shot down the lake. I was hanging on for dear life while Kathie was able to enjoy the experience riding in my sled. The trip was wonderful. Bright blue sky, white snow, and the only other sound was the dogs barking as they pulled us over the trail. We made our way into Basswood and stopped for lunch on the ice. Billy had brought some fishing gear, and after drilling holes through about 36 inches of ice, we put out our lures while the brats were cooking. We caught a couple of average-sized Northern Pike but released them before heading back at the end of the day. We learned a lot about the sport that day and enjoyed watching how the dogs would interact with each other. If they got tired, one would slow up to smell some "yellow" snow, and before you knew it, they were all taking a break. A great day and a special experience we'll never forget.

During the off-season, we also enjoyed day trips to the Northshore. Northshore was the term used for US Highway 61 that went from Duluth to Canada along the shores of Lake Superior. It was a beautiful drive with small towns, shops, and numerous restaurants and resorts scattered along the route. We would travel from Ely over MN Highway 1 to reach Lake Superior. It was a narrow road with many turns though heavily wooded areas along several small lakes, beautiful, especially in the fall. A typical trip would take us along the shore to Grand Marais. This was a quaint town with a restaurant we loved, Birch Terrace, that sat on a low hill overlooking the lake. It was a wonderful escape from the routine of our business, and on more than one occasion, we had to dodge deer and on a rare occasion, a moose as we traveled home.

Myrtle Beach

In the late 1990s, we decided to take a real vacation. Our last one had been our 25th in Florida some ten years earlier. Barb and Gary had sold out and were working in Myrtle Beach. Pressure from all that they'd been through finally caused them to go their separate ways, but we thought it would be fun to spend some time in Myrtle Beach, SC. Barb worked as a booking agent for a large ocean-side resort and was able to secure us good rates for our stay. Jim, Kim, Corri, and Colton joined us. As sort of an afterthought, I invited the "gang" from DC to join us, and to our pleasant surprise, we had an impromptu Rusk reunion. Mike and Jill had already planned a Florida trip so didn't participate. We flew in from Minneapolis, and everyone had a wonderful time on the beach. We all agreed to continue these reunions in the future.

PART 6: "IS IT TIME TO SELL?"

In the late 1990s, a series of events occurred which, when put together, started us to consider the possibility of selling the resort.

Bob

As you probably understand, our dog Bob was a major part of our lives at the resort. We were totally involved with him, and he responded by always being able to pick up our spirits whenever tough times were encountered. As the years rolled by, he became our "old man," loved by everyone. In the mid-90s, he started showing signs of failing health, and the vet decided he had testicular cancer. We had him neutered, which resolved the problem, and after recovering, he returned to his normal self. However, after his 16th birthday, things started to go downhill. Hearing was failing as well as his sight. We had to watch him closely around the kids, as his not being able to hear them, they could surprise him. One evening while visiting Jim and Kim, he nipped Colton, and we think that is what happened.

For anyone who has had a pet for such a long time, you know how hard it is to say goodbye. Bob reached a point where at times he couldn't control his bowels, and Kathie and I started to talk about allowing him to "go." One morning when he didn't return from his walk, I found him curled up in a small hole next to Cabin 5. As animals do, he had found a place to die. We took him to the vet that afternoon. In all his years visiting the vet, Bob never allowed anyone to put him on the table. However, this time he did not object, and we said goodbye.

What wonderful memories we have of Bob. I've already mentioned some of his actions, but there are many more. He never enjoyed riding in a vehicle. Guess he got scared when he was a pup. On our trips to Indianapolis, he would suffer in silence. Never sleeping and shaking a lot of the time. He also hated overpasses and would duck when they passed. He enjoyed walking with us. Running ahead and back and forth into the woods. When something got his attention, he would jump straight up in the air like a gazelle. What a character. One day he got a little too exuberant coming out of the woods taking Kathie's feet out from under her. She landed on her tailbone and suffered for quite a while. On another occasion, he confronted a deer by our garage and before we knew it, the deer had chased him under the garage, and we had to come to his rescue. He also had a distinct "Bear Bark." More of a low growl followed by a serious bark. He could smell them from inside the house, and we always knew when one was coming in to "attack" our bird feeders, a favorite target. Knowing that he would go right after the bear, I never let him out when one appeared. And finally, at the end of the day, he would sit next to my chair, and I would pet him, and he leaned against me like saying, "well, we made another day."

I think part of the resort died along with Bob. Our guests sent cards and one even arrived the next year with a headstone in his honor. We never did attempt to replace him, and I really believe some of our spirit for the resort business left with Bob.

Internet

In the late 1990s, the Internet became a strong factor in our business. As more and more people turned to it to find vacation sites, attendance and interest in the Sport Shows waned. We started to see fewer potential customers, and the handwriting was on the wall that we needed to develop an internet site to remain competitive. I had spent a lot of time with the Chamber developing its website and had met a man who was quite good in the field. I hired him, and together we designed our site. It turned out to be a very good site, and we even got it to a point where each cabin was highlighted with individual photos, floor plans, etc. Once we had the site up and running, we decided to stop attending the Indianapolis Sport Show. While we hated doing that, it was simply not cost-effective.

I never did like using the website. While it generated numerous email inquiries, it didn't allow for personal contact between us and the potential customer. I think a lot of folks, bored at work, would simply surf the Internet without really being that interested in vacationing in our part of the world. Thankfully, our solid base of repeat customers kept us going, but things were beginning to change in our business, and I was, quite frankly, uncomfortable with the changes that I was seeing.

My Back

For some reason, the boys were unable to come and help cut wood in the spring of 1999. We had just hired a new young man to help named Josh. He turned out to be a real problem. Looking back, I should have fired him a week after we hired him but didn't. We had to advertise for the position, a first, and the market for such help was tight so we didn't let him go. Big mistake. He was one of those types that if he didn't like cutting grass, he'd run the lawnmower over a rock and then complain that it wouldn't work. Kathie also caught him huffing spray paint down in the boat house one day. Again, I didn't fire him. What a dummy I was!

We had to have wood, so I ordered the normal ten cords. I realized that I could not trust him to run the chainsaw so that would be my task. We worked for over a week on that wood. At the end of each day my back would hurt but I wrote that off to the chainsaw plus all the bending to split the wood, etc. There is an old saying that you move a piece of wood 17 times from the log to the fireplace. That is true, and all of these movements require heavy use of your back.

After we got the wood done, my back continued to bother me. I also had some trouble walking and fell more than once. This really aggravated me because I always prided myself on being able to walk well through the woods, etc. One thing I'd learned from Ranger School so many years ago was to let your feet find their own way; it worked, and now it didn't. I had no idea what was going on. A few weeks later, I suddenly started getting shooting pains down my legs. When it happened, it was like an electric shock and would nearly knock me off my feet. One-night things came to a head, and I was in so much pain we had to call the doctor. He prescribed Vioxx. It worked quite well, at least reducing the pain to where I could get around. Walking long distances became very difficult and Kathie suddenly had to do my work as well as her own. The doctor had me undergo an MRI and prescribed physical therapy. Fortunately, the summer season was over. The initial reading of the MRI was "old age with normal wear and tear." Physical therapy did not help, and I revisited the doctor. She asked me to walk across the room on my heels and to my amazement I could not. My right foot would not lift up and in effect just "flopped." She said it was time to see a surgeon and made an appointment for me in Duluth.

The neurosurgeon was a great doctor. He immediately diagnosed my problem as stenosis in my lower back. He also said there was evidence of an old compound fracture and wondered if I had ever been in the Airborne. Quite amazing. Stenosis was the buildup of bone on the vertebra which in turn caused pressure on the nerves thus creating my pain. The surgery would remove this bone and relieve that pressure. There was no question in my mind that I had to do this, and surgery was scheduled for that fall. By now I was in such a state that I could only obtain relief by walking bent over. In a supermarket I would push the cart bent so far over I could not read what was on the top shelf.

Kathie and I spent the night in a hospital motel in Duluth and then walked over in the morning for the surgery. It all went well, except that there was a long delay in getting me from the recovery room to my room. Remembering what had happened to Mike, Kathie was quite upset thinking the worst. Later that day I got up from the bed and Kathie exclaimed that I'd grown six inches. I was standing up straight for the first time in several months. The surgery proved to be quite successful except for some strange feelings in my toes. After an overnight in the hospital, we headed back home, and my recovery went quite well. Looking back, I still am less steady on my feet because of all of this, and my feet became very sensitive. I'm sure this is a direct result of nerves being damaged by the event.

To Sell or Not to Sell

In 1999, Jim began to make suggestions that it was time to sell. We were now in our 60s, and the work wasn't getting easier. That summer, with my back problems, Kathie had been worn to a frazzle. I could tell this as at times she would get "short" with our guests, something neither of us had done. The guest was "always right!" I really didn't want to sell. We were only a couple of years away from making our last payment on the resort, plus I had no idea where I wanted to go if we did sell. Jim was lobbying hard for Indianapolis, but I wasn't sold on the idea. A great location to work but not to retire. We thought long and hard about what to do. I slowly started to realize that the spark that had driven us all these years was beginning to dim. I was dreading seeing a customer walk up to our house, thinking what kind of problem now? I still kid Kathie that I decided to sell because one day she told a guest that "maybe the problem wasn't with the fish but with the fisherman," I suddenly knew it was time.

In January 2000, we contacted a local real estate agent that specialized in resort sales. Most resorts were taking anywhere from one to two years to sell, so we thought we would give the sale idea a shot for a while, knowing we could always drop the plan. I also decided to take a lesson out of the old realtor's playbook and only include 30 acres with the resort, keeping 40 acres for us plus some lake frontage down the river. We also stated we would only accept a cash sale and would not owner finance any sale, still a common practice for resorts. We signed the paperwork and went about our business thinking nothing would happen.

About two weeks later, our agent brought a couple out to look over the resort. They never really looked much beyond our house. We had a nice conversation and thought nothing about the visit as they drove out. A couple of days later the agent called saying he had an offer for the resort. We were stunned. Did I put too low a price? What was happening? As with any transaction we went through an offer/counteroffer process, and would you believe sold the resort to the first people that had looked at the place. We negotiated in good faith, agreeing to certain covenants such as allowing the new owners to manage the road as most remained in our possession. Our plan was to sell off the remaining land and we agreed, in good faith, to allow the resort owner to charge new property owners a "reasonable" fee for road maintenance. We also got them to agree to allow an electrical easement to any new property owner as the power line ended at the resort. These negotiations would come back to haunt us in future years.

The new owners wanted to be in before the season started so a closing date of May 1 was agreed upon. Suddenly we had 60 days to decide where we were going, prepare for the move and then actually move. By now we'd decided to move to Indianapolis and took a trip there to make plans for where we'd live.

Jim had the idea that we could build an addition onto his house. They had a large lot, and we went so far as to contact an architect who did a couple of concept drawings for us. Finally, we decided not to go this route as the resulting home would be quite difficult to sell and maybe being so close was not a good idea. Thankfully it would soon prove to be the correct decision. Indianapolis had several garden style home areas designed for retirees. We found that we really liked the way the houses were designed and started looking seriously at these developments. The wife of one of Jim's police friends was a real estate agent and she took us around to compare various areas. We finally settled on a small place in Plainfield, a small community just west of Indianapolis. After all those years in a small one-bathroom home, we were easily sold on a two-bathroom place! It was almost twice as big as what we'd been living in, so we knew we'd be comfortable.

Returning to the resort we had many things to accomplish. Weeding though things that would make the trip to Indianapolis and those that would remain at the resort. The sale also required us to list all the property that was included in the sale. All the furnishings in each cabin, boats/motors, etc. I had a nice 16 foot fishing boat which I decided to keep, and I also kept a new outboard motor for Jim. The list ended with a canned saying "plus other items too numerous to list," This turned out to be a good idea.

Closing went very well considering all the stories of other closings. When Jeff and Lori sold it took all day for the closing as the new owner continually raised questions that had been resolved during the negotiations. The only strange part was the owner's insistence that their nine-year-old son also sign all the closing documents. Another curious item was that they never asked for an inspection of the property. We had anticipated such an inspection and expected a long list of items that needed correcting before the sale was finalized. For whatever reason they choose not to do that and later that too would become a "bone" of contention between us.

We were suddenly staring at a large check and needed to make decisions on how to invest those dollars. Over the years, I have been good at buying when prices in the stock market were high and selling when they were low. We made a good decision by turning to the Edward Jones Company for investment advice. Their agent was a member of our Rotary Club, so I felt comfortable with his advice and counsel. It was early 2000, and stocks, particularly "tech" stocks, were breaking price records almost daily. The temptation was there to dump the money into Mutual Funds holding such stocks. However, I wanted a steady return on my investments throughout the year to help offset expenses that I knew were before us. We spread the dollars between interest-paying bonds, an annuity, and one mutual fund.

When the market bubble for technical stocks blew up later that year, I suddenly looked like a genius as my significant investment in bonds protected us from losing significant dollars. We also made the decision to buy Long-Term Care policies for each one of us. We still own them and while we hope we will never need them believe that such policies could make a huge difference should one or both of us end up in a nursing home. We had learned from Hilda's experience.

We rented a U-Haul truck, and since we needed to stay a couple of extra days after closing, I flew Jim and Tom up to drive the truck back to Indy. They also towed my boat which worked out well. We stayed in Cabin 6 for a couple of days writing individual letters to our returning guests explaining the sale and asking them to give the new owners their best. The owners were thrilled to see us leave. A preview of things to come.

Indianapolis/Move In

Our home was in a small housing development called Crystal Bay. Most of the homeowners were retired or preparing to retire and had "downsized" when they moved into the area. It featured a small lake that was really a pond by Minnesota standards. We were not on the lake, but I hoped that I could enjoy a little fishing, especially with grandson Colton. The development would also be our first involvement with a thing called a Homeowners' Association (HOA). The move-in was quite funny. We left the boat at Jim and Kim's house, and then Jim arranged for a bunch of his police officer friends to meet us at the house to unload. They all brought their police cars, and suddenly the small community had five police cars surrounding the house. It took the better part of an afternoon to finish the job, and by then we had quite an audience of new neighbors watching. I learned later that one neighbor had even questioned one of the HOA board members about what kind of people were moving into the neighborhood.

Once we were settled, Jim and I started looking for a pickup truck large enough to tow the boat. Jim found a small Dodge in pretty good shape, and we had our truck. A couple of weeks later we decided to bring the boat over and try the little lake at Crystal Bay. There was a small launch ramp. Prior to putting the boat into the lake, I researched the HOA rules and regulations about boating and asked for and received a sticker for the boat. Only trolling motors were allowed on the lake. My boat had a 40hp gasoline motor, but we kept everything associated with gas out of the boat and proceeded to start fishing with Jim and Tom. The big motor was not in the water. About 30 minutes into the trip, we had one homeowner rush down to the lake yelling that we were not allowed. I showed him our sticker and ignored him. When we finally finished our brief two-hour trip and returned to the landing, another guy was there yelling. He identified himself as a HOA board member saying that my boat was not permitted. When I questioned the regulations and pointed out that we'd only used the trolling motor, all I got were four-letter words. We left. I went to the next board meeting and demanded an apology plus requested that if a boat like mine wasn't allowed then they should change the regulations. The regulations were changed but I never received an apology. I was left with a sour taste in my mouth towards the community and the HOA. We never fished in the lake again.

One thing we decided on was that we wanted to travel. In addition to our plow truck, we had relied on first, a Ford Escort sedan and later an Escort station wagon for our personal transportation. The vehicles were "stick shift" due to the need for traction during the winter months. Once we were settled in, it was time to look for a new vehicle and we decided to look at higher-end sedans. Our search led us to many funny incidents. We looked at Lincoln, Chrysler, Toyota, and Lexus models. I will always remember driving into the Toyota dealership. Usually, as a prospective buyer, a salesman would appear immediately. However, when they saw our Ford Escort, they suddenly had other things to do! We did manage a test drive but after much searching decided to buy a new Lincoln sedan. The Lincoln salesman told us that it was the first time the dealership had taken an Escort as a trade-in. We were proud of our new acquisition and of what we had achieved during our career at Northern Lights Lodge.

The Resort

Shortly after our arrival, we started receiving letters and telephone calls from the new owners. They wanted this and that paid for. One claim was for over $1,000 to take property we'd left at the resort to the dump. I, of course, refused and finally won that argument thanks to a phrase in the property list, "other items too numerous to list." The next claim was for a new roof on the house. We knew the roof needed replacing and assumed that would be part of the results of the inspection they had not asked for. My initial response was, "you bought it, you can fix it." They then accused me of not listing all the wells on the property, required by Minnesota law, and after checking, sure enough, I had blown it. I had forgotten two Sandpoint wells, one of which had saved us. They said that they would go to the State if I did not replace the roof. After consultations with my lawyer, I reluctantly agreed to pay them $3,000 for the roof.

Soon friends were telling us that they were telling everyone in the area how we had deceived them during the sale. We were quickly learning what type of people they were. Guess that's life. On the one hand, I loved them for paying cash and on the other hand, they truly upset both of us with their antics.

We still had 40 acres of land left to sell and one of my first tasks was to have the land along the lake surveyed and listed by a local realtor. Once that was done, the owners started playing their tricks. For Sale signs suddenly disappeared from our lot and I received a four-page letter from them threatening to call the sheriff should any realtor appear on their property. What a mess! Then we learned that when prospective buyers toured the land, they would intercept them and tell them about the "road association costs." As I have mentioned earlier, I gave that right to them in support of their right to conduct business. Now they were using that right to stop my efforts to sell the property. Prospective buyers were told that they would be required to pay at least $1,000 every month for road maintenance. In the 19 years we owned the road we had never spent $12,000 to maintain the road. It was a very strange situation that caused both Kathie and I to lose lots of sleep in the coming year. I had offered them the extra land at the time of sale plus they had the "Right of First Refusal" on every sale. I guess the bottom line was what they told Jeff one day. We would never sell anything, and they would have "free use of our land." It was like they had planned all of this from the very beginning. Amazing!

Trying to sell the land dragged on for over a year and then suddenly I had multiple offers. We accepted one which promptly fell through over the road maintenance issue. Both the realtor and I were frustrated over the situation. Finally, a new buyer appeared, and I sweetened the deal by offering to pay the first year's maintenance fee plus added some dollars for electrical service and the deal was finally closed. The owners did not exercise their right to buy the property, which really blew me away. We sold the land for less than $150,000 and they could have easily broken the land into two lots and sold each for $150,000 making a 100 percent profit.

I then hired a different survey company and had the remaining 28-plus acres cut into four parcels. By now, Lori was involved in real estate, and we contracted with her to be our agent. Again, whenever she put up a For Sale sign it would be ripped down and thrown into the woods. Based on our original sales agreement, the new owners were required to provide an electrical easement for me as well as the folks that bought the lakefront parcel. Even though the properties joined each other, the new owners again delayed everything by developing plans for future development trying to block and/or lengthen the electric easement. Another attempt to disrupt my efforts to sell the property. After months of arguments and legal fees, they backed down and provided the necessary easement.

Our easement ran down the road and across that little creek I talked about earlier. I knew that should I try to run power that way I'd encounter resistance. The owners had trouble with the DNR for replacing the old culvert without the proper permits and I knew they would make sure those few feet of "wetlands" would become an issue. Therefore, I sought an alternative route. The closest was from a pole on the Timber Wolf property. I talked at great length with the new owner, walked the proposed route, and got what I thought was his agreement for an easement. Based on this, we surveyed the route, got our lawyer to draw up the paperwork for the easement, and sent it to him for signature. No response. I would call and get no answer and my messages were not returned. That summer we visited Ely and Kathie and I confronted the owner. He hemmed and hawed and finally said "no" to the easement. We could do nothing without the easement. Another $2,500 down the drain.

One last route remained. Along Highway 21 and down our road to the various lots. We had the work done at a cost of over $25,000 and a few months later we had an offer on a second parcel.

Selling multiple parcels was a complicated matter under Minnesota law. Laws were on the books designed for developers, requiring such things as platting to include installing wider roads, etc. I had no desire to invest that sort of money. However, the law also said that a person could sell one lot per year without platting. This is the route I selected, and Lori and I made very sure that there would only be one transaction per year. The folks who wanted to buy the second parcel went to St. Louis County to ask questions about a building permit.

The office refused to grant a permit saying that I was only allowed to sell two lots per forty acres which I had already done. My buyer immediately backed out, which we understood. Again, more lawyer fees and no resolution of the problem. I was suffering from two problems. First and foremost, I believe, I was an out-of-state resident and no one in county government was willing to make a judgment call. Secondly, the county government consisted of small "fiefdoms" where the boss could make unilateral decisions without repercussions. My only recourse was to list the remaining three lots as one parcel.

Looking back, it's obvious to the reader that I made several errors negotiating the resort sale. I guess I could use the excuse that the sale came so quickly that I was unable to do advance thinking concerning several issues that came back to haunt us in later years. I think it was also the fact that I was too trusting. While we were honestly trying to help them with the conversion of ownership, they were operating on their own agenda. Sometimes, "you get the bear, other times the bear gets you."

T-dock on the beach

Cabin #4 – Let's go fishing

Cabin #4, new screen porches

Let's go swimming!

Mike and Jill's wedding

Jim and Kim's wedding, Hilda and Bill

New fishing boat plus arrows in the tree

Mike's happy return from surgery

Our new cabin #6

Jim's 50th birthday with size 50 Bra

Son Jim, Grandson Colton (CJ) This is how you do it!

Kathie and Mother, Hilda in Cleveland

#1 Cozy 1 bedroom cabin. Ideal for a honeymoon couple. Located on the water with a view like the front of our brochure. Features a 3-season porch which is fully carpeted with a double sleeper sofa. Ideal for 2 or 3, can accommodate 4. Interior redone in 1990.

#2 Large 2 bedroom cabin capable of sleeping 6. One double and two twin beds in the bedrooms with a double sleeper sofa in the living room. Huge 20' x 8' 3-season porch overlooking the lake. Interior redone in 1991.

#3 Spacious 2 bedroom cabin. Ideal for 4 or 6. One double and two twin beds in the bedrooms with double sleeper on porch. Features a huge 30' cedar deck and 3-season porch overlooking the lake. Interior completely redone in 1990.

#4 Large 2 bedroom cabin capable of sleeping 6. One double and two twin beds in the bedrooms with a double sleeper sofa in the living room. 20' x 8' 3-season porch overlooks the lake. Our most private cabin. Interior redone in 1991.

#5 Huge 3 bedroom cabin capable of sleeping 8. 2 bedrooms have one double bed and the other has two twin beds. A double sleeper sofa is in the living room. A large 3-season porch overlooks the lake. Interior redone in 1991.

VALUE FOR YOUR VACATION DOLLAR!!

Description of cabins/amenities

Northern Lights Lodge

Bear Island Lake   Ely, Minnesota

1991 Rates
HOUSEKEEPING CABINS
(One, Two and Three Bedrooms)

Cabin No. 1
Weekly rate for two
(1 Bedroom) $310.00

Cabins 2, 3, 4
Weekly rate for two
(2 Bedroom) $360.00

Cabin 5
Weekly Rate for two
(3 Bedroom) $385.00

Each additional person.....................................$45.00
Each child under ten $30.00
Children under 2 yrs $20.00
Overnight Guests (per day) $15.00
Daily Rates: 1/5 of Weekly Rate

Well mannered, controlled pets welcome.

One Boat Per Cabin

Check in time.................................Saturday, 2:00 PM
Check out time ....Saturday, 9:00 AM
Rates subject to applicable state and local taxes.
$50 Deposit required with each reservation.

NORTHERN LIGHTS LODGE

FOR RESERVATIONS CALL COLLECT OR TOLL FREE
218-827-2501 (Collect)
Toll Free 1-800-777-4406

Price list from 1991

EPILOGUE

After a few more years, things settled down between us and the new owners of Northern Lights Lodge. We were also able to negotiate with St. Louis County on another parcel sale, which left us with a final 27-acre parcel. The resort remained in business, and in 2020, the Minnesota YMCA bought our parcel, the resort, plus the neighboring resort, Timber Wolf Lodge. It is now operated as a YMCA camp, retaining the name Northern Lights. We visit whenever we return to the area and are happy to see folks continuing to enjoy our small piece of "heaven" years after we left.

Our time in Indianapolis was spent enjoying our grandchildren. We did the normal things with Corri and Colton, enjoying time in Jim and Kim's pool during the summer, babysitting when asked, and generally enjoying retirement. We were given the titles of "Oma" and "Opop" by the kids. Mike and Jill also adopted their first daughter, Ruby, from China in 2004, and her arrival into the Rusk family was a time for great celebration.

We both felt that Plainfield would not be our final retirement location. The Indianapolis area was a wonderful location to work and raise a family, but it was also hot and humid in the summer and cold and wet in the winter. We ended up spending parts of three winters between Florida and Arizona. Much to our surprise, we discovered that we enjoyed our time in Arizona much more than Florida. In 2004, we made the decision to move to Green Valley, Arizona. The decision was a hard one as we would be leaving our boys and their families. That fall, we bought our new home, and after selling our place in Plainfield, we made the move to Arizona in the summer of 2005.

We are enjoying our retirement and our journey through the twilight years of our lives. I remain active in Rotary and continue to receive a sense of fulfillment working on many projects. We have also become active members of our church and have served in leadership positions within the church. We especially enjoyed the fact that no one was born and raised in Green Valley. Everyone settled here for their retirement years, and we all enjoy making new friends. In April 2024, we will celebrate our 62nd wedding anniversary.

Both boys have remained in Indianapolis. Mike and Jill adopted their second daughter from China – Luna – in 2006. Jill is an ovarian cancer survivor, which prevented them from having children together. Both have enjoyed successful teaching careers in the Indianapolis area while raising Ruby and Luna. They will celebrate their 27th wedding anniversary in May 2024. Ruby will graduate from Manchester University in May 2024 and continue her work towards a medical degree. Luna will enter college in the fall.

Over the years, Mike has continued to recover from the aneurysm, achieving new plateaus and overcoming the physical challenges associated with his surgery. His life became fulfilled with his marriage to Jill and their subsequent adoption of Ruby and Luna. His empathy towards his elementary school special needs students has also contributed to this feeling of satisfaction. While eligible for retirement, both he and Jill have no plans to do so soon. He celebrated his 60th birthday in June 2023.

Jim and Kim parted ways in 2004. Both worked together over the years raising Colton and Corri. Colton enlisted in the Navy and has been a submariner for the last 6 years. He and his wife, Bailey, are assigned to the Naval Submarine Base in Groton, CT. Corrie graduated from DePauw University in Indiana with a degree in Communications. She played four years of college volleyball, ending her career as team captain. She is now working in the business world in Indianapolis. Jim found his life partner, Wendy, and retired in 2023 after 32 years with the Indianapolis Metropolitan Police Department. Jim and Wendy own a small business and are looking forward to complete retirement at some point.

We love to visit Minnesota whenever possible. For three years, we rented a college apartment in Duluth during the summer and one summer stayed in a student apartment at Vermilion Community College in Ely. The visits allowed us to enjoy the area without the responsibilities of our business. Jim and I also made two, weeklong trips, into the Boundary Waters Canoe Area. A wonderful way to again experience the joys of our little piece of God's country.

God

I have always believed that a person's relationship with his/her God is a private matter. Some folks embrace him openly and vocally, while others do it in a quiet, almost peaceful manner. I am not sure where I fit in but mostly towards the quiet side. One of my biggest turn-offs are those "Born Again" who suddenly say, "It's their way or the highway." I believe in being content with your God, trying to live right, and allowing others to follow your example rather than your rants.

One of my biggest regrets is that I did not take more time to expose the boys to religion. I was always too busy or there was football on Sunday.

Thankfully, Michael found God on his own. I firmly believe that his faith has carried him through his health challenges over the years. If you reread Part Three about Mike, you can clearly see God's hand at work throughout his recovery. We discussed religion and he was concerned about my feelings towards the subject. I would like to share part of a letter he wrote to me on August 18, 1996. "John 3:16. "For God so loved the world that he gave his one and only son, Jesus Christ, that whoever believes in him shall not perish but have eternal life." This morning 'the pastor' was talking from Isaiah 40. Verses 28-31 that really spoke to me. "Do you not know? Have you not heard? The Lord is the everlasting God, the Creator of the ends of the earth. He will not grow tired or weary and his understanding no one can fathom. He gives strength to the weary and increases the power of the weak. Even youths grow tired and weary and young men stumble and fall; but those who hope in the Lord will renew their strength. They will soar on wings like eagles; they will run and not grow weary; they will walk and not be faint." Mike ended the letter by saying "this is an important decision for every person to make."

Kathie

I started this book with a dedication to my wonderful wife, Kathie. It is most fitting to end it with a final "Thank You." I am sure you now understand that my journey through life would have been quite different without her love and support. Somehow, despite all my rants and wild decisions, she was my "rock," standing beside me, always supporting me. As the book was put together, we had many long discussions about items covered in the book. It might have been dates, locations, facts, or perceptions. Overall, I believe it was a fun journey for both of us. I only hope that our journey together will continue for many more years. Once you have finished the book, sit down with her, and she will tell you what really happened!